MW01102084

A COSTLY STAND

My husband's brave and lonely fight for justice against his powerful bosses at Hollinger

By Mary Lynn McCauley Winkler

To Bud
The best
real estate
agent ever.
Enjoy retirement!
Mary Lynn + Paul

A COSTLY STAND

ISBN-10: 1495418723 / ISBN-13: 978-1495418723

1. Memoir – Journalism – Business Ethics

Cover and interior design: Jim Szeplaki, J & S Graphic Design
Photography: Cody Chase

Printed by Createspace
Second Printing June 2014

Published by PAJE Publishing
1070 Deborah Street
Fonthill, ON
L0S 1E4

Additional copies can be purchased by contacting Paul or Mary Lynn Winkler
pwinkler@vaxxine.com
(905) 892-9582 or (905) 687-0015

DEDICATION

To the memories of Paul's mother, Elizabeth (Betty) Winkler, whose strong faith Paul truly admired, and to Morgan Fisher, a high-school business teacher who had a profound impact on Paul's life.

To my parents, Thomas and Marjorie McCauley, who instilled in me the virtue of always telling the truth.

To our children Patrick, Andrew, Elizabeth, and Jake Winkler.

ACKNOWLEDGEMENTS

We are truly grateful to those people who testified at Paul's trial and risked their careers to be his witnesses.

Thanks to our immediate and extended family and friends who supported and encouraged us; especially dad, who read our early drafts and motivated us to persevere. We owe a debt of gratitude to our former Trajan Publishing business partners and friends Anderson and Susan Charters as well as Andrew Hanon for taking time out of their busy schedules to read and make valuable suggestions to our manuscript.

For his sage legal advice, we thank Daniel Henry.

Finally, we owe a great amount of thanks to our extraordinary editor, Susan Chilton. Her thorough editing and guidance helped us create a clear, tight narrative. Without her expertise, publishing this book would not have been possible.

PROLOGUE

We are writing this memoir to document for our children, and for anyone else who reads it, how crucial it is to tell the truth, to act with integrity, and to maintain trustworthiness within family, friend and work circles. This is a tale of being morally courageous, taking a stand, and staying true to one's values and principles. It is a narrative of how my husband, Paul Winkler, stood alone in his effort to expose misdeeds by the top brass at Hollinger, one of the largest newspaper companies in the world. Some compared Paul's battle to the biblical David's, a young shepherd boy whose rock, propelled by a slingshot, knocked down the enemy's giant soldier, Goliath. Yes, Paul was a little guy up against a big corporation, but that's where the analogy ends. We wish Paul's battle could have been as quick and as final. Taking down his Goliath involved years of legal proceedings and then a dogged campaign to alert securities authorities and the media about what Paul saw as immoral, devious and sneaky business practices.

Recounting this forced us to relive the experience, which proved to be cathartic. We share in these pages how we, as a family, bounced back from adversity, and how, through the process, we demonstrated to our children how to stand up to corporate bullies. This memoir explains why we took a stand, and why we stayed true to our values and principles.

Everyone has a story to tell. We are not unique by any means and we realize that there are stories far more traumatic and heart-wrenching than ours. What is unique about our experience is how long it dragged on and how we coped with seemingly being punished for making the right moral and ethical decisions. My husband made a bold and brave decision late in 1999. It turned our world upside down and took all of us, including our four children, on a tortuously long roller-coaster ride.

Paul suspected his employer, a company owned by Hollinger*, at that time chaired by CEO Conrad Black and his partner, David Radler, of some serious wrongdoings. Paul refused to participate in business plans that he deemed underhanded. These men didn't realize who they were up against. In his youth, Paul wanted to be either a police officer or a detective. When he sees a wrong, he wants to right it and he will not back down. During his tenure as president of the Ontario Community Newspaper Association in the mid '90s, Paul helped uncover a serious case of white-collar crime. He spearheaded its resolution. It makes him chuckle, but he has been compared to the late Jimmy Stewart for his role in Mr. Smith Goes to Washington, a movie about a man who finds himself in the middle of a corrupt political scheme.

This memoir is a collaborative effort. Paul's story revolves around factual and historical events, mostly from 1996 to 2004. Mine is the narrative of the deeper, emotional experiences surrounding those events.

When Paul's career was cut short, he was only 46. Our wounds were fresh and raw, but time has mellowed us, and taken the sting out of them. During our recovery process, we have witnessed some justice served and we have pursued new career paths. We have emerged triumphant, strengthened in character, closer as a couple and a family, and ever more trusting in our faith and belief in the truth.

* Throughout our book, Hollinger means Hollinger International Inc.

CONTENTS

INTRODUCTION

"Why did you leave?"

We have been asked this question countless times since we moved from the sunny Central Okanagan region of British Columbia back to smoggy and humid southern Ontario.

I sometimes respond that it's too complicated to get into, while Paul is able to fill people in with a quick and precise summary. The longer, more drawn-out version has often made for interesting dinner-party conversation in Fonthill. Our friends have commented, "You should write a book," or, "That would make a good movie."

Writing about our experience has not been as simple as telling our story to acquaintances over a bottle of wine. Our original intent was to collate the myriad of notes, court documents and media articles into one scrapbook for our children. We committed to publishing, though, after Paul received positive feedback on his presentations on Business and Ethics to leadership groups, service clubs, and schools in the Niagara Region. Paul's talks to these groups in Niagara reveal that his messages on business ethics, the need for social responsibility and transparency, resonate more deeply than ever.

THE CONRAD BLACK EMPIRE

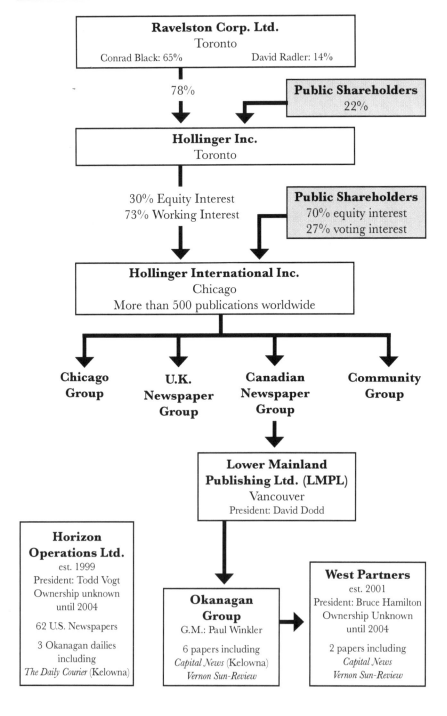

Ravelston Corp. Ltd.
Toronto
Conrad Black: 65%   David Radler: 14%

78%

Public Shareholders
22%

Hollinger Inc.
Toronto

30% Equity Interest
73% Working Interest

Public Shareholders
70% equity interest
27% voting interest

Hollinger International Inc.
Chicago
More than 500 publications worldwide

Chicago Group

U.K. Newspaper Group

Canadian Newspaper Group

Community Group

Lower Mainland Publishing Ltd. (LMPL)
Vancouver
President: David Dodd

Horizon Operations Ltd.
est. 1999
President: Todd Vogt
Ownership unknown
until 2004

62 U.S. Newspapers

3 Okanagan dailies
including
The Daily Courier (Kelowna)

Okanagan Group
G.M.: Paul Winkler

6 papers including
Capital News (Kelowna)
Vernon Sun-Review

West Partners
est. 2001
President: Bruce Hamilton
Ownership Unknown
until 2004

2 papers including
Capital News
Vernon Sun-Review

I

LIVING IN PARADISE

*"We write to taste life twice, in the moment
and in retrospection."* - Anaïs Nin

It was the evening before my 40th birthday, at the end of March 1998. We were cleaning up after dinner and my husband Paul and our four children were struggling to lure me away from the kitchen sink. Marriage and motherhood transformed me in odd ways. Housework, specifically vacuuming and scrubbing pots and pans (never laundry, dusting or ironing), had become my de-stressors. The kids helped with chores, but I was always there to pitch in and explain cleaning techniques.

Paul knew I also really enjoyed long walks. To pry me out of the kitchen, he begged me to go for one that night, even though he much prefers to run. Our oldest son grabbed the vacuum, while the other three quickly started loading the dishwasher and snatching tea towels to dry. I reluctantly acquiesced. I sensed something was up.

On our walk, Paul and I marvelled at how well our move to Kelowna, British Columbia had gone. We were transplanted Ontarians now living in what we thought was paradise. Paul was thoroughly enjoying his new job as general manager of a group of community newspapers in the Okanagan Valley. As we strolled along the streets in our neighbourhood that early evening, he was basking in the success of the re-launch of the Capital News, which had taken place about six months prior. It was "textbook" he said enthusiastically, adding that all the stakeholders were

1

happy. The owners loved the profitability, employees were energized and having fun, more locals were turning to the Capital News for their local information, and advertisers benefited from the increased readership.

It was great to see Paul so energized and passionate about the newspaper business again. He left Kitchener, Ontario in October 1996 to start his new job as the general manager of Lower Mainland Publishing Limited's Okanagan Valley group of community newspapers. Then he became the temporary publisher of the group's largest publication, the Capital News, about five months after his arrival. I was relieved he was enjoying his new job because his work environment back in Ontario had become acrimonious as the years waned. We were experiencing a little bit of heaven.

We returned from the walk and Paul searched for the kids, who were nowhere in sight. He ran downstairs and called me, in a distressed voice, to come quickly. I felt a sense of panic as I raced down the steps to see what the matter was. "Surprise!" my neighbours shouted when I opened the door to the recreation room. I was thrilled, but a bit embarrassed, because I was dressed in my grubby clothes. I was wearing a T-shirt that Paul got when he worked for Southam Newspapers in Ontario. In response to CEO Bill Ardell's charge of mediocrity at the papers, some disgruntled daily newspaper publishers (not including Paul) had T-shirts printed that said, "Who cares, after all we're only mediocre." Well, the party was far from mediocre. We had a wonderful night and it seemed that my forties would be fabulous. Little did I know.

II

A FRESH START IN A NEW LAND

"Life is a process – just one thing after another.
When you lose it, just start again." - Richard Carlson

When I first arrived in Kelowna, it was the snowy, cold winter of 1997. I love skiing and was thrilled to get up to Big White, the second biggest resort in B.C., within weeks of arriving. Sitting on a chair lift, my shoulders hunched over, my hat, coat and even my face covered in a light, white frost, I could hardly make out the terrain below me through the fog. Even though I was scared out of my wits at the thought of navigating a mountain I could barely see, I felt exhilarated.

Our four children and I had finally joined up with Paul, who had started his job the previous October as the general manager of LMPL's Okanagan group of community newspapers. We six were once again all under one roof living in Kelowna, a city many consider to be the most idyllic in Canada.

The Okanagan Valley region is a national treasure. It contains Canada's only official desert and the country's warmest freshwater lake. Summers are long, hot and dry, boasting the highest number of hours of sunshine in the country. Massive Okanagan Lake abounds with private and public beaches. It even has its own Loch Ness monster – the serpent, Ogopogo. The mild winters in the Okanagan are a dream to southern Ontarians. Fall days are fragrant, the air heavy with the scent of the many wineries' grapes. Spring is glorious, especially April when the hills become a sea of white and pink, as blossoms bloom on the apple and cherry trees.

We lived away from the lake at higher elevation, on what they call the "benches" in southeast Kelowna. Each and every time we drove down McCulloch Road, the main route to the core of the city, we were fortunate to experience the most spectacular views. Around one of the bends in the road is a bird's-eye view of Harvest Golf Course and a panoramic scene of the valley. If ever I were in a bad mood, it changed when I came to that curve in the road.

The Okanagan Valley runs north-south between the Cascade and Monashee mountains. It's a popular spot for many summer vacationers and a dream area for many retirees. When we lived there, at the turn of the new millennium, Statistics Canada reported that Kelowna had a growing and a disproportionately large number of seniors compared to other communities in the country. From a business perspective, Paul was rightly excited about his future there. The geography of the area offered protection from competing media, and retirees still read newspapers.

I love to travel and to experience new things. However, as a part-time journalist and mother of four children then ranging in age from two to 10, moving was daunting, even if it was to paradise. Still, after the stress of staying behind to sell our house, the mayhem of packing over the Christmas holidays, and a turbulent flight, we were there.

My ski companion, Paul Fiocca, was sitting with me on the chair lift that foggy day. Fiocca was a close family friend and operator of Trajan Publishing, a small St. Catharines company of five hobby magazines that we owned with him and another couple. Fiocca was politely listening to me explain a few of Paul's business strategies for the Capital News. I felt nervous and apprehensive, yet oddly excited, about what was to transpire at the paper under Paul's leadership. Change, no matter how justified, is seldom embraced.

"Oh, you mean there's trouble in paradise," Fiocca mused, puffing on a cigarette, as the chair lifted us yet higher through the pea soup.

In retrospect, that day's conversation and the dark, gloomy weather conditions were harbingers of things to come. Our trouble would be more than we could ever in our worst nightmares have imagined.

III

THE PAST SHAPES OUR FUTURE

"Everything depends on upbringing." - Leo Tolstoy, War and Peace

Paul had lived in Kitchener all of his 43 years by the time we moved to the Okanagan Valley. I, however, had left Kitchener in 1977 at the age of 19, to live in Nantes, France as an au pair. In 1978, I enrolled in Carleton University in Ottawa for four years. I worked at Standard Broadcast News on Parliament Hill for a year and a half. I then experienced Toronto for a while before moving back to Waterloo Region to resume work at the Cambridge Times, where I had spent two summers as a journalism intern, and where I first met Paul.

So, when Paul got this opportunity to be the general manager of the Okanagan group of papers in October 1996, four children and a massive move aside, I said, "Sure! That sounds great. Let's go for it!"

The timing was good. In the spring just prior to the Okanagan job offer, Paul had come to the conclusion that his job at the Fairway Group in Waterloo Region and Brabant Newspapers in Hamilton had become virtually impossible. They were at war with their own sister daily papers: The Kitchener-Waterloo Record and the Hamilton Spectator, both also owned by Southam.

It was only going to get worse. Conrad Black's Hollinger had recently taken control of the parent company, Southam. Black had already purchased the small dailies in Cambridge and Guelph from Thomson. Paul figured that Hollinger would take steps to reduce his ability to compete in those markets, too, knowing that Hollinger liked to make money with small dailies in non-competitive markets. After almost 20 years at the helm of Fairway and six at Brabant, Paul felt it was best to move on. The writing was on the wall.

His newspaper journey and sense of foreboding might appear complicated to those not familiar with the industry. Paul's career had humble beginnings. He started out in 1972 as a proof boy in the advertising department at the Kitchener-Waterloo Record, then privately owned by the Motz family. At 18, he made $65 a week. He was offered an outside sales position, but left the paper after a year to enrol in a broadcasting course at Conestoga College in Kitchener. People had told him he had a great radio voice. However, when he found out the remote places he'd have to move to earn a meagre living in broadcasting, he quickly dropped out.

Paul's business sense is about as natural as breathing. Perhaps it had something to do with his upbringing. His father died suddenly when Paul was eight; his brothers seven and two. Widowed after only nine years of marriage, Paul's mother was forced to raise her three boys with very little money. She grew up on a farm outside Stratford, Ontario during the 1920s and '30s. After elementary school, she begged her father to let her continue her education, but she was told she had to stay home and work the farm. Her experience during the depression as well as the little money she had after her husband died, most likely spurred her to record in a ledger every purchase made, even an ice cream cone. Since Paul's mom didn't have a car, her groceries were delivered to the house. Paul recalls well how she painstakingly reviewed the receipt item by item. If she were overcharged, she'd discuss it with the cashier on her next visit to the store. Most importantly, if she were undercharged by more than a few pennies, she would send one of her boys back to the grocery store, about two kilometers away, to return the money.

"We didn't have a car, didn't go on vacation and often drank powered milk because mom couldn't afford the real stuff. She did a spectacular job under very difficult circumstances. I was determined to climb out of poverty and make mom proud," Paul remembers.

Paul's strong moral streak was due in large part to his mother's child rearing style. Although Paul's mom and her three sisters did not attend church growing up, they joined an evangelical church on their own as young adults. When she married Paul's dad at age 30 — he was 41 — they both attended his church, St. Matthew's Lutheran in Kitchener. As children, Paul and his brothers weren't allowed to go to movies since his mom's evangelical church didn't approve. There was no alcohol in the house and gambling was strictly forbidden. The Winkler boys not only attended Sunday school and church service every Sunday morning, they often went to a church service the same evening, in Stratford, with relatives. The best part of church, Paul readily admits, was Boy Scouts. St. Matthew's was home to the highly successful 20th Kitchener scout troop. Paul spent almost 10 years in the Scout movement and developed a deep love of camping and outdoor activities.

Like all young kids, he ran lemonade stands. But, unlike most, he didn't stop there. At 12, he and his brother, David, started a chain of comic-book stands. They branched out into costume jewelry – he tells me he still doesn't know where the jewelry came from. At 16, when most guys are ogling girls, Paul and a friend turned their sights to wholesaling record albums, posters, tie-dyed T-shirts, and other 1970s paraphernalia. He and his friend travelled in a van throughout beach country – I'm sure they noticed the girls – peddling their wares in those communities.

In his final year of high school, Paul won the Kitchener-Waterloo Sales and Advertising Club's annual top student award for academic and enterprise initiative. He credits his success to Morgan Fisher, a Cameron Heights high-school marketing teacher who died in 2013. Fisher had given up a successful business career to teach. Paul kept in touch with him throughout his own career and considered Fisher his mentor.

During that time, Paul also spearheaded an unusual venture that had a substantial impact on the community. In 1969, he became a founding member of Sing-Out Kitchener-Waterloo, a group formed by Up With People, an American non-profit singing organization. Teens and young adults performed musical numbers for various political, business, and charitable functions. In the summer of 1972, Paul did some public-relations work for Up With People in Burlington, Vermont. He co-founded The Project People Show in Kitchener in 1973, after the Sing-Out group disbanded. This non-profit organization was a glitzier, Las Vegas-style show consisting of 30 singers, dancers, and musicians. The group was a regular at major Toronto conventions as well as fairs, exhibitions, and political gatherings throughout the province. Clients even flew The Project People troupe to Vancouver and Montreal. Paul gave up his managing duties in 1983, after a 10-year tenure.

His full-time job still was, and had always been, in newspapers. After his brief stint as a broadcasting student, Paul was hired as a sales rep for the Cambridge Times, a weekly under the Fairway community newspaper umbrella. By 1974, he earned $110 a week. At 23, after taking the Dale Carnegie course, Paul was promoted to sales manager of the four Fairway newspapers. A year later, through a chance meeting with the owner, Paul Motz, he was asked to write a report on how to make the Fairway papers economically viable. Motz wanted the money-losing chain revitalized through innovations. Paul threw himself into the project without the aid of any financial statements. He proposed a decentralized model that eliminated his own sales manager job. He figured that he was going to leave anyway; why hold anything back? To his shock, Motz liked his plan. He asked Paul to execute it and named him the publisher of the Fairway Group. Paul was 24 years old.

In the same year, 1978, Paul formed a partnership with two friends and his brother to start up a go-cart track at a local entertainment park called Eat 'N Putt. It was a lucrative business, to say the least. Sadly, it lasted only five years. The Eat 'N Putt property was expropriated by the provincial government in 1983, to allow the construction of a new highway. This forced the partners into a legal battle with the Province of Ontario. Paul and his partners won their case and were awarded damages of about $100,000. Their legal fees were over $100,000, but they were fully paid by the government because it lost. This was an early lesson for Paul about how important it is to take a stand when you know you're right.

In his full-time job at the Fairway Group, Paul decentralized the operation of the papers from being head-office controlled to having a general manager at each location. He believed strongly in the concept of "intrapreneurship" (a spirit of entrepreneurship in a corporate environment). The papers showed dramatic improvements. In the early '80s, Fairway launched several new magazines, including Exchange Business Magazine, a glossy lifestyle publication called Highlights (later Kitchener Waterloo Magazine), and a tourist digest magazine, Visitor. There was also a division focused on producing flyers for shopping centres throughout Ontario and a creative department. A seniors' magazine came later. These were exciting times, but there were always complications sharing an owner with your chief competitor, the local daily. The Kitchener-Waterloo Record had been the core business for decades and, while no one wanted to do any economic damage to it, clearly the growth was with Fairway.

In 1987, at the age of 34, Paul was appointed president of the Fairway Group. This was more of a formality, because he and Bob Davis, long-time general manager of the printing division, had worked as a team. We had been married for three years and had been blessed with the birth of our first child, Patrick. By this point in his career, Paul's business philosophies and beliefs were well entrenched. He surrounded himself with smart, keen and enthusiastic team members, established profit sharing and set goals that were attainable with hard work. He had a reputation as a fair, but tough-minded, boss. He also made it known that he had a strong dislike of "victimitus": people who blame someone or something else for their problems.

Growing up Catholic, I had the privilege of being taught by nuns. There weren't too many of them teaching in the Catholic system in Kitchener by the time I graduated from St. Mary's, an all-girl high school. A nun who taught me in Grade 2 gave me the impression that she valued only quiet, studious students. When asked to explain my low mark in conduct, she told my parents that I was a social butterfly. I admit that I did like to chat, but that most likely helped me win the vice-presidency on my high-school student council.

After Grade 13, and after living in France for a school year, I returned home a much wiser and more grown-up young woman. While studying at Carleton, I worked as a summer intern at the Cambridge Times, where I met Paul. About one month after graduating with my Bachelor of Journalism degree, I got a job as a secretary/cub reporter at the Parliament Hill Bureau of Standard Broadcast News, a radio news service.

Paul and I started dating seriously. I moved back to Waterloo Region in 1983, and was hired by Al Coates, who was then the editor and publisher of the Cambridge Times. Paul and I married in November 1984. While raising our two sons, Patrick and Andrew, I worked at Fairway part-time. Indeed, it was difficult to be working with staff when your husband is the "big" boss. The tension was too much for me, so I elected to become a part-time journalism instructor at Conestoga College. I taught a feature-writing course, managing to complete the year just in time to give birth to our daughter, Elizabeth, in 1991. For the next five years, I continued to do freelance writing assignments. In 1994, I gave birth to our fourth child, John, affectionately known as Jake.

In 1989, the Fairway Group had added the Guelph Tribune, a weekly that essentially had been started by the Kitchener-Waterloo Record, but had been turned over to Fairway after its unsuccessful launch. Politics were always a factor between The Record and Fairway since they shared a common owner and were direct competitors. Paul felt Fairway should have been given the job to launch the paper from the outset. Partly out of that frustration, we put everything we owned on the line and became financial partners in Trajan Publishing. Paul was hopeful Trajan would grow and eventually provide him an employment opportunity.

In 1990, the Southam newspaper chain purchased the remaining 52 per cent of JEMCOM, the Motz-owned parent company of the Kitchener-Waterloo Record, the Fairway Group and two other businesses. Paul then reported to Russ Mills, president of the Southam Newspaper Group, instead of to Paul Motz, fourth-generation owner of the K-W

Record. Mills' group was first and foremost a daily-newspaper operation, disinterested in community newspaper groups such as Fairway. Southam had also recently acquired the Brabant community newspapers in the Hamilton area, strictly to keep it from falling into the hands of a fierce competitor.

Southam Inc. was a publicly traded TSE 20 company, one of Canada's 20 biggest publicly traded corporations. It owned most of the largest newspapers and trade magazines in the country. It also owned Coles bookstores. Southam was going through considerable changes at the top. Paul witnessed this. He had four different bosses in six years and saw 14 of the 16 daily newspaper publishers leave during the same time period.

Within days of the announced sale of the Fairway Group to Southam, Tom McCarthy, the publisher of the Southam-owned Brabant papers, based in the Hamilton area, decided to shut down his printing plant. He told general manager Bob Davis and Paul that he was hopeful that Fairway could handle the extra business.

"Bob and I were over the moon with delight," Paul recalls. "We'd need to put on a third shift, but adding this amount of new business would clearly enhance our profits."

Their elation soon turned to outrage and frustration.

"Brabant had roughly 100 full-time employees, and was the only fully unionized community newspaper group in Canada, and probably North America. A company that was marginally profitable under private ownership became a big loser under Southam ownership."

The work environment under former daily-newspaper executive McCarthy was acrimonious. He and the union were constantly at loggerheads. After announcing that he was closing his printing plant and moving all of the printing to Fairway, he did a 180-degree turn. He talked the executives at Southam head office into funding a new facility in a building privately owned by Wilson Southam, a member of the founding family.

What followed was awful for Fairway. Despite Paul's protests, he was told that the script for the annual meeting had been written and that the Fairway printing plant was going to close, moving all of its work to the new, consolidated plant run by Brabant. Paul was also told not to worry; his future with Southam was bright.

McCarthy had to hire a host of additional press helpers for his new press operation. Some were recruited at a local bar. "Chaos" would best describe what followed, as the presses didn't run on schedule and quality was a problem. Soon after, McCarthy was transferred and Paul was asked by Mills to take on Brabant, too.

Paul developed a strategic business plan and Mills approved it. As he had done before, Paul re-organized the business from centralized to decentralized. "We turned it around from a business losing millions into one that was modestly profitable," Paul says.

These were the days when, much to his chagrin, Paul got his feet wet in dealing with unions. Early on, he had developed a deep-seated dislike for unions, although he understands why they came to be and the good they did early on. Paul's brother, David, worked at the post office in Kitchener for many years, during the time when there were many postal strikes and militant actions. Postal workers made considerable money in those days. In fact, David made more as an inside postal worker than Paul made as publisher of four newspapers, at least early in his career. It wasn't just the amount of money they made that was an issue for Paul. David's stories of bizarre behaviour from some of his co-workers would have resulted in being fired at any non-union shop, but not at the post office.

Paul believes that to succeed, you need a strong work ethic. That, combined with serving the needs of others, is, in simple terms, what makes the free-enterprise system work. Most good employees are valued, but in rare circumstances, they are not. If that's the case, Paul believes they should move on to a place where they will be appreciated. As an executive, Paul found that many of his experiences with unions ran contrary to his work philosophies.

In his brief time with Southam, Paul learned about what seemed to him to be crazy agreements that management had made with unions. "There's a saying that the industry adopted from academia's 'publish or perish.' In our case, if we stop publishing, someone else will quickly fill the void. Daily newspaper publishers made a ton of money back then. Rather than take a tough stand with their unions, they often capitulated to outrageous demands just to keep publishing. Things like jobs for life," he relates.

Paul heard of some pressmen who were no longer able to perform their work, but were paid as long as they showed up. Some, who were in their seventies, came to work and played cards every day. There were stories of union members getting severance pay at death and presses that wouldn't run unless the electricians, who maintained them, got overtime pay for having worked through their lunch. "These were the issues many of my fellow Southam publishers were dealing with, but in community newspaperland, the publications and presses I operated had to run like a real business, not the bloated public utility that the dailies had become."

Paul did a certain amount of battle with Peter Murdoch, who at that time was chief negotiator for the Southern Ontario Newspaper Guild (SONG). Paul took pride in the fact that his employees were among the highest paid in the community-newspaper industry. The profit sharing he had engineered had boosted their incomes even further. This didn't matter to the union bosses, who also acted for the employees at the big dailies. They wanted Fairway and Brabant wages to be comparable to wages paid at the dailies owned by Southam.

Paul soon learned that the path to union peace was to let the union paint you as the bad guy then, at contract negotiation time, be sure you're prepared to "grudgingly" offer them some goodies. "Then they can claim victory to their members," he says. Paul would often say about Brabant, "We have seen the enemy and it is us." It was dispiriting for him. He felt he spent more time dealing with the union and internal problems, including underachieving personnel, than he spent building the business.

Soon after Bill Ardell was appointed CEO of Southam, Mills went back to run the Ottawa Citizen. Following a reorganization, Ray Elliott took over some of Mills' portfolio. Eventually, Ardell appointed John Craig, Southam's long-time chief financial officer, to head up the trade magazine division (Business Information Group) along with the non-daily papers, including Fairway and Brabant. Paul enjoyed working with Craig. For the first time in his career, he didn't report to the person who was also responsible for the dailies in his markets.

Ironically, this change led to Paul's departure. Craig suggested that Fairway start a paper in Kitchener. Paul and his management team were eager to try it, because it would mean that Fairway had a network of papers that, when combined, were delivered to virtually every home in the entire marketplace. This would be a huge competitive advantage. It would impact the daily paper, The Record, but that was something Paul was told he didn't have to worry about. His brother, Peter, who had been running Fairway's Cambridge paper, was selected as publisher of the new Kitchener product. Months of planning culminated in leasing space, hiring staff, and making presentations to major advertisers. Management at The Record was outraged and did everything possible to stop the new paper. That included convincing the other dailies in the Southam chain to lower their prices to major advertisers if the advertiser agreed not to advertise in Fairway's new Kitchener paper.

Ardell called Paul to Toronto and told him it had been the most difficult business decision he had ever had to make, but the new Kitchener paper had to be scrapped because it would have too much impact on the daily. If that was the case, Paul didn't see how he could continue to lead Fairway and told Ardell it was too much of an about-face. The launch was just days away. Ardell spoke to Craig, who called Paul to say that the paper could go ahead if the plan were re-written stating the competitor was the Pennysaver (a chain of shopper papers), and that Fairway would not go after The Record's advertisers. Craig re-wrote the plan, but Paul declined to sign off on it, saying it would be disingenuous.

The Kitchener This Week paper launched, but its mere existence continued to be the subject of countless meetings and a parade of consultants. The straw that broke the camel's back for Paul came when the head of Southam's dailies, Andrew Prozes, recommended that the best way to minimize damage from too much competition was to let the dailies have control over all of the large advertisers. Fairway's papers would have all of the small advertisers; variety stores were cited as an example. The same solution would be applied to Paul's other group, Brabant Newspapers in the Hamilton area. There, the Hamilton Spectator would get all of the large advertisers. This ridiculous, inequitable suggestion was the final blow for Paul.

Almost 20 years earlier, when Motz promoted him, he had told Paul to run Fairway as if Paul owned it himself. Paul, who had worked long hours, had personally tried to buy the Fairway and Brabant publications, but that wasn't possible. Under Paul, Fairway publications grew from $1-million per year in revenue to $8-million, without any acquisitions. He had turned a long-time, money-losing business into a successful operation. He had even managed to get profit-challenged Brabant into the black.

"I had faced many obstacles along the way, but had never been told I couldn't compete for business. After considerable reflection and discussion with Mary Lynn, I went to Craig and suggested it was best if I were to leave. This was tough because I was about to be given a third chain of papers to manage, the newly acquired Rannie Group from the Niagara Region. I suggested that Southam treat me, severance-wise, as well as the daily newspaper publishers they were getting rid of, and promised to stay on for a number of months to aid with the transition."

Craig understood Paul's dilemma and arranged an amicable parting. He asked Paul to do some consulting work with a suburban Edmonton chain of community papers for his remaining time with Southam. Southam owned a share of this chain along with a partner, Duff Jamison. Jamison's family had owned the business for decades. After spending some time with Jamison, Paul went to British Columbia to check out a newspaper operation in Kelowna. He then travelled to Vancouver to meet with Southam's partners in a company called Lower Mainland Publishing Ltd. LMPL was a big and fast-growing chain of community papers and related businesses, mainly located in suburban Vancouver. Southam owned 62 per cent of LMPL and Madison Partners owned 38 per cent. Madison had operating control over the business, though, because the Competition Bureau didn't want Southam having too much control over the newspaper market in the greater Vancouver area. It already owned both daily Vancouver papers, The Vancouver Sun and The Province.

Craig wanted Paul to meet with the senior executives at LMPL. Craig knew they were looking for someone to head up their expanding operations in B.C.'s interior, based in Kelowna. Paul went out in June 1996. He called me and described the beauty of the area and how fresh and fragrant the air smelled. He said he couldn't believe he was in Canada, because it had a more southern and exotic feel to it. Little did we know that it would soon become home.

IV

THE BIG TURNAROUND

"The greater the difficulty, the more glory in surmounting."

- Epicurus

It's amazing what a fresh start in a new province, and a job with a different company, can do for a motivated person. After almost two decades of running the Fairway Group, a regional community newspaper, and magazine publishing company, Paul needed a change. In Kelowna, he felt rejuvenated, ready to tackle anything, and his business creative juices were flowing.

As the general manager of LMPL's Okanagan group, Paul oversaw six papers: The Vernon Sun, Shuswap Sun, Merritt News, Enderby Commoner, Lumby Valley Times, and the Capital News. The last was housed in a beautiful building in Kelowna and included a printing press. Paul was told there would be an opportunity to buy into the group after some corporate issues were resolved. This was very enticing, because Paul had tried unsuccessfully to buy into the operations he had run in Ontario. With LMPL, he also signed an employment contract for the first time in his life. That contract would come into play in the years ahead.

Paul has an innate ability to fix things that are broken. He focused his attention on the Capital News, which published three times a week and was the largest of the group's papers. The competing Thomson-owned newspaper, The Daily Courier, was subscribed to by less than

30 per cent of households. Paul knew that the Capital News had the potential to be a dominant force in the media market and to attract more advertising in the process.

He spent the first few months assessing the marketplace, management, and his new staff. Kelowna was a crowded media market with a seven-day-per-week daily, a TV station, and five radio stations. In its early days, the Capital News had been a shopper (an advertisements-only publication), but it had evolved into a newspaper. It was afforded that opportunity because the competing Daily Courier had a history of strikes.

Paul says, "The problem with the Capital News was that most local people didn't see the paper as much more than a shopper. They loved the big classified section, TV listings and flyers, but the news was largely ignored even though the paper had a nine-person newsroom." He saw the potential, but needed to make some internal changes first.

That became abundantly clear in February, just one month after the children and I arrived. Paul and I were invited to the home that Jim Clark, then the publisher of the Capital News, shared with his partner, Vera Stewart, the head of accounting for the six papers. Paul recalls, "I came into a bit of a messy situation in Kelowna and had been prepped by the owners in Vancouver, who also saw opportunity, but were also unsure of what to do with local management.

"Clark, who was patriarchal and protective, had a group of loyal managers around him. He had run the paper and printing operation for the previous independent owner, and wasn't a corporate-type guy. His relationship with Vera was a concern for the new owners, too."

We were joined at Clark's by several other Capital News managers. Everything was fine until Clark started drinking and bad-mouthing people, particularly the new Vancouver owners. Clark even had a nickname for LMPL. He called it "Limple."

"As the drinks flowed, most of the managers started chirping in support of Jim's views, making it very uncomfortable for me as LMPL's newly hired regional manager," Paul recalls. "At the end of the evening, when we got in the car, I said, 'They all have to go.'"

Paul's desire to make management changes became even greater after a rather peculiar event. "A copy of The Globe and Mail was delivered to Jim Clark as the publisher," Paul remembers. "I was used to reading it and suggested to Jim I look at the paper after he was finished with it. One morning, he was late arriving to work so I grabbed the paper, read it, folded it back up and returned it to his desk. The next day, two Globes arrived, one with Jim's name and one with my name. In my surprise, I asked Jim if he had ordered me the paper. He said he had and I replied that we didn't need two papers. To that, Clark bluntly stated, 'I like my paper crisp.'"

Getting rid of senior management is tricky and costly unless they are fired for cause, and that's not easy. Somewhat to Paul's delight, Clark sent a letter suggesting that he had been constructively dismissed. Paul and his new bosses didn't agree with him, but it did open the door for a negotiation. Paul suggested a pre-arranged severance agreement for both Clark and Vera Stewart. Clearly, both were uncomfortable with Paul and his new role. He proposed that he and they try working together, but that any of the three of them could trigger the severance at any point over the next several months. Within weeks, Clark and Stewart bailed, paving the way for further changes.

"The owners agreed with my suggestion that I assume the role of publisher, temporarily, and lead the changes. Karen Hill was the second-ranking person in accounting and someone Vera had threatened to let go. I don't remember why Vera felt that way, but Karen stepped in as business manager and did an outstanding job."

Bryden Winsby was the long-time editor of the paper. He was also Clark's closest confidant and occasional drinking buddy. Staff respected him and considered him to be a steadying influence. Paul knew the paper needed a different editorial approach and design, and was hopeful he could convince Winsby to make changes. Paul hired Ken Bosveld, an editor and publisher from Ontario, to come out and spend time with Winsby in an attempt to gain his support for change. It was not to be. Winsby, too, departed.

Fortunately, news editor Andrew Hanon, who had pretty much run the newsroom anyway, was eager to lead the upcoming content and design changes, and more than capable.

The rest of the management team included Richard Sadick, the advertising manager; Alan Monk, the Real Estate Weekly manager; Stuart Cook, the national and regional advertising manager; Gary Green, the classified manager; Tessa Ringness, the production manager; and Al Fradette, the press manager. Glenn Beaudry was soon added to the team when his business, Flyer Delivery Service, was bought out by the paper.

Paul invited in three other easterners as consultants: Donna Martin, a leader in desktop-publishing; Len Kubas, one of Canada's foremost retail and media researchers; and Fred McLean, a business planning and human resources expert. McLean was hired to work with the management team to help create a strategic and operational plan.

Sadick, the paper's advertising manager, was the one wild card on the management team. Although he had been very loyal to former publisher Clark, Sadick was well connected to the community. On the surface, he exuded the typical qualities of a strong salesperson. He was confident, outgoing, assertive, funny, and cared about his customers. However, he switched his allegiance and support from Jim Clark to Paul so quickly it set off some alarm bells in Paul's head. He wondered whether smooth-talking Sadick was sincere in his support or merely the type who would do whatever he had to do to succeed. Paul knew he would have to use all the tools in his management belt when dealing with Sadick.

It was great to see Paul having fun at his job after the six final tumultuous and rocky years under Southam in Ontario. Our neighbours were welcoming and outgoing, and the children had settled in well at South Kelowna School. It's amazing how popular you suddenly become when you move to a destination city. Our first summer there was filled with visitors. I would literally say goodbye to one set, then quickly clean and change bedding for the next. We had overnight guests 90 times that year. Paul was enthusiastic not only about these family members and friends, but about inviting business consultants and industry experts, too. I like entertaining, but I was becoming overwhelmed.

That first year in Kelowna was very tough on me, emotionally. I felt like I was an island, disconnected, alone and cut-off from my network in Kitchener. I felt bitter and I cried easily, which is completely at odds with my cheerful personality. Paul was having fun and I wasn't. I was a stay-at-home mom who really wanted a job – and not as a Bed and Breakfast operator, which is what I felt I had become. I was a journalist; Paul could have arranged for me to be a writer for the Capital News. However, he believed I should get the job on my own merits, prove myself, and go through the proper interview procedures with the editor. I was annoyed, but I knew he was right.

On top of all of that, our youngest son, Jake, was diagnosed with asthma and a plethora of food allergies. Let the strict food regimen begin. I was a B&B-operating Doctor Mom.

Paul and I talked about my feelings of anxiety and isolation and he suggested counselling. That was hard for me to accept, because admitting weakness is difficult for me. Nonetheless, I gathered my courage and took the plunge. It was the best thing I ever did. My counsellor helped me uncover the root of my discontent: feeling responsible for the problems of people close to me. Once I let go of other people's problems, and talked to Paul about that in later counselling sessions, life changed and so did our marriage. In retrospect, it was also good that I took that counselling, because it helped us cope with the curve balls life would soon throw at us.

By the spring of '97, Paul had his team in place. In the months that followed, strategic and operational plans were established. Focus-group sessions were held with community leaders and advertisers to get their feedback about how the Capital News could be more pertinent. Meetings were also held with the newspaper staff to elicit their opinions. Paul hired the highly regarded Angus Reid company to do a broad survey of the readership, media and shopping habits of the marketplace, too. All of this culminated in a re-designed, re-focused paper, full of new content that bore little resemblance to the former paper.

"The whole team was justifiably proud of what had been accomplished. The feedback was excellent and it felt great having the whole team rowing in the same direction," Paul says.

V

PAUL SMELLS A RAT

"The only thing necessary for the triumph of evil,
is for the good to do nothing." - Edmund Burke

Our nightmare started innocently enough in late spring 1998, when word came that an ownership change was expected for LMPL. The company had two shareholders: Madison Partners of Vancouver with 38 per cent, and Southam Inc. of Toronto with 62 per cent. Operating control was and had been with Madison, the minority shareholder, because of an issue with the federal Competition Bureau. Most of LMPL's papers were in the Greater Vancouver marketplace, where Southam owned both daily papers, The Vancouver Sun and The Province. The Feds didn't like one company owning so many papers in one market. A resolution had now finally been worked out, paving the way for Southam, then controlled by Conrad Black's Hollinger, to take over LMPL.

Hollinger had grown to become the third largest newspaper chain in the world, owning most of the biggest dailies in Canada along with hundreds of mostly smaller U.S. titles. It also owned England's prestigious The London Telegraph, as well as The Jerusalem Post. CEO Conrad Black had become one of Canada's best-known citizens. His media empire had given him a platform to not only comment on world affairs, but associate with many of the most influential business and political leaders on the globe. He was granted life peerage in the British House of Lords, with the title Baron Black of Crossharbour.

Hollinger's takeover of Southam, the company Paul had worked for in Ontario, was part of Paul's reason for leaving. He wasn't too concerned with Hollinger as owner now because the circumstances in the Okanagan were considerably different than what he faced back in Ontario where the competition often came from daily papers that shared the same owner. Paul's B.C. operations were showing big improvements against real competitors.

David Radler, Conrad Black's long-time business partner, maintained a low profile in public but was the man who ran most of the expanding empire. His job titles were many and included Deputy Chairman, President, and Chief Operating Officer of Hollinger. He was also publisher of the Chicago Sun Times and both Vancouver dailies, the Sun and Province. Radler had earned a reputation for being ruthless, with a singular focus on making money. Much of Hollinger's success came from the hundreds of smaller papers it owned. The formula was pretty simple: own papers in non-competitive markets, such as Cranbrook, B.C. and Mammoth Lakes, California, and cut expenses to the bone to ensure healthy profits. After all, where else could readers and advertisers go in a monopoly?

Paul also knew that Black didn't bother with the small papers. This territory belonged to Radler, whose practice was to visit each one, usually just before the acquisition took place. Right on schedule, just prior to Hollinger taking control of LMPL in late 1998, Paul got to meet the infamous Radler, a man described by award-winning author Peter C. Newman as the toughest-minded executive he had ever met. That's saying something, because Newman had met just about every prominent Canadian executive over the past 50 years, while writing his many articles and books.

"I was told Radler would be arriving at the Kelowna Airport about noon," Paul remembers, "but to my surprise, I received a phone call first thing in the morning saying Radler had changed his plans. He would be landing in minutes and I was to be there to pick him up. The airport was a short drive from my office, so I dashed off. When I arrived, I discovered the short-term parking lot was under construction, so I was forced to drive farther away to long-term parking. I wasn't too concerned, though, because I didn't see a corporate jet in the area reserved for private planes. I thought they were late.

"Imagine my surprise when, upon entering the arrivals area, I was greeted by one of Radler's 'lieutenants,' who demanded to know why I was late. Unbeknownst to me, the pilot had parked their large Challenger jet in the commercial airliner section, telling authorities they'd just be there for a brief meeting. They stayed most of the day, though, and I later heard through the grapevine that airport management was miffed.

"In any case, Radler refused to deplane until my car was right at the gate. He came off the plane with a cell phone in hand, briefly acknowledging me. He explained he wanted to go to Vernon, a small city just north of Kelowna, where LMPL had a relatively new, twice-weekly paper up against a very strong three-time-weekly owned by David Black, a highly successful, independent owner of newspapers based in Victoria. And, no, David Black is not related to Conrad Black. Anyway, this was not part of the plan and I tried to dissuade Radler, but to no avail.

"The publisher and ad manager in Vernon each had an equity stake in the money-losing paper. It was an arrangement that wasn't working and changes were needed. I must admit, however, I was amused when I saw the look on their faces when the receptionist retrieved them from a smoke break out back, explaining that David Radler was there to see them."

Paul's first impressions of Radler were mixed. Radler is rarely quoted and seldom photographed by the media. He stayed in the background, while his partner, Black, was front and centre. Paul says that Radler, who was short, seemed to have a permanent tan, which wasn't surprising because we knew he had a home in Palm Desert, Calif. His family and main office, though, were based in Vancouver.

Paul often told our friends and family about the meeting that took place in that Vernon newspaper office. "It was one of the most bizarre meetings in which I've ever been involved. Radler sat down in the publisher's office and put his feet up on another chair. At one point, he turns to my soon-to-be new boss, David Dodd, and asks rhetorically, 'Why are we in business, David?' Dodd responds with something like, 'To increase shareholder value, Mr. Radler.'

"Radler says, 'No, we don't give a *(expletive)* about shareholders.' He then turns to Bob Calvert, the executive in charge of most of Hollinger's papers in Western Canada, and asks, 'Bob, why are we in business?'

"Bob says, 'To make more money for ourselves.'

"Radler responds, 'David and I have more than enough money and you're getting there, Bob. No, we do this to have fun with people like David Black.' Then, with a weird twinkle in his eyes, he brings his thumb and forefinger together as if to squeeze the life out of a tiny insect. It was like a scene from a really bad B-movie.

"On our way to the Kelowna office, Radler orders me to stop at a seedy-looking motel. I find out he owns it and he wants to do a surprise inspection." Radler clearly likes to catch people off guard.

Just after the surprise inspection, Paul and his three guests went for lunch. Paul crowed to Radler about the gains the Capital News was making at the expense of The Daily Courier. Paul explained that he believed high quality two or three time per week free community papers could put small dailies out of business. He recounted how in Ontario his Fairway Group's Cambridge Times, a free paper, prevailed over the daily Cambridge Reporter.

Paul recalls, "You'd think Radler would have been pleased to hear my positive outlook for our paper in Kelowna but what he said to me set off alarm bells. Radler told me in a very matter of fact way that I was 'fucking full of shit.'"

Philosophically, Paul and Radler had different approaches to making money in smaller newspaper markets. Conrad Black's partner preferred to make money with daily newspapers, the majority of which were in smaller markets. For his part, Paul loved to compete against those newspapers since they were often unionized and vulnerable to aggressive competition. Paul figured Radler didn't mind dealing with unions since most of his papers were virtual monopolies, which allowed him to take a strong stand in negotiations.

While travelling in the car, Paul told Radler that he was still interested in acquiring the Penticton Western News, owned by Sun Media. The paper was already part of a group buy, providing advertisers with access to virtually every home in the Okanagan Valley. Radler didn't have his own cell phone, so he had either Dodd or Calvert dial Paul Godfrey, then Sun Media's president. Radler left Godfrey a message saying he wanted the Western added to the list of papers he was buying from Sun Media. Just like that.

Paul remembers finally arriving at the Capital News building, where he had a spacious, sunny corner office with large windows. He had read that Radler fired publishers whose offices were bigger than the men's washroom, so he made sure to inform his future bosses that he had inherited his ample digs.

Paul gave his entourage a tour of the fairly new, two-storey building, built by the paper's previous owner. It housed a printing press, but all Radler remarked was that "half the building is devoted to play," after seeing the staff lunchroom and second-storey patio.

"A meeting was held with the management team and Radler," Paul resumes. "The biggest issue facing our business was the recent announcement that David Black of Black Press might purchase the money-losing Daily Courier in Kelowna, and its sister daily, The Penticton Herald. He would then own papers in the three Okanagan Valley cities and would have a competitive advantage over us. Radler explained to our managers that Hollinger was a $2-billion operation and David Black's was only $80 million."

Paul remembers thinking, "OK, Hollinger is bigger, but how does owning The Jerusalem Post in Israel help us in the Okanagan?"

Even less relevant was Radler's offer to have well-known Chicago celebrities, such as syndicated movie reviewer Roger Ebert from the Hollinger-owned Chicago Sun-Times and Sammy Sosa from the Chicago Cubs baseball team, come to Kelowna to help with the upcoming battle with David Black. It seemed to Paul that Radler was simply name-dropping.

"The meeting ended and I took my guests back to the airport. We drove by the Radler-owned motel and, as we did, he told Dodd to make a note to arrange to have the big tree out front removed."

We can't remember if the tree came down, but by December 1998, the sale of the remaining LMPL shares, and with them operational control, were with Hollinger. Although Paul had left Ontario in part to avoid working for Southam/Hollinger, the circumstances surrounding their ownership in Kelowna seemed better than they had been back east.

David Dodd was now Paul's boss. A tall Brit with a military-style brush-cut, Dodd was an accountant by trade. Paul called him "the field general" because he had a commanding presence and excelled at following the orders of his long-time boss, Radler.

On November 28, 1998, soon after the deal closed, Paul sent a letter to the exiting LMPL president, John Collison. He copied it to his new boss, David Dodd. Paul wanted to be on record confirming that the role he was in as publisher of the Capital News was temporary. Soon after, Dodd called Paul requesting he fly to the Vancouver airport so they could meet there on January 21, 1999. He wanted to discuss Paul's plan for the highly competitive Vernon market.

David Black's Vernon Morning Star, published three times weekly, had the highest percentage readership of any newspaper in the country. Virtually everyone read it. It had successfully killed off the Thomson daily several years earlier, using a formula similar to what Paul wanted to do in Kelowna. "Our (Hollinger) Vernon Sun paper was an economic disaster. The publisher and ad manager were former Morning Star managers who thought their personal connections would help them steal plenty of the Morning Star's business," Paul explains.

That didn't happen. The publisher departed and the ad manager was promoted to publisher. The plan was to turn the paper into a more upscale product with more in-depth reporting, because the paper had a strong investigative reporter. Paul explained the proposed positioning of the product to Dodd, who was intent on having the paper turned into more of a shopper. He called it a "market spoiler." None of this made any sense to Paul at the time, but it did in the months that followed. Paul countered that his plan was too far developed and that to go in the opposite direction would cause great harm, indicating that a shopper wouldn't market well with the other papers in the group. Selling the entire Okanagan market to an advertiser with similar products would be a key strategic advantage, Paul insisted. Dodd reluctantly agreed.

Dodd then informed Paul that there was a hiring freeze, and that no employees who left any of Paul's papers could be replaced. That was perplexing, because Paul's operations were booming, but Dodd phrased it in such a way that it sounded like a chain-wide decision. When Paul got back to Kelowna, he checked with several other LMPL publishers in the Vancouver market and discovered they were under no such freeze. Something was up, but what?

At the January meeting in Vancouver, Dodd sloughed off Paul's concerns about Paul's own role, saying, "Don't worry Paul, we need good managers." He told Paul, in very matter-of-fact language, that Paul would either learn to accept the way Hollinger operated or Paul would leave. Paul certainly left that meeting with a far-from-warm feeling about the man to whom he now reported.

A few weeks later, Paul connected with his friend, Dale Brin, the publisher of the Kamloops Daily News. Brin was also a good friend of Bob Calvert's. Calvert ran Hollinger's smaller dailies in Western Canada and reported to Radler. In confidence, Brin told Paul that he heard Paul would soon be asked to take over from Dodd as the president of LMPL. About a week later, Dodd called Paul asking him if he would move, should the right opportunity arise. Paul replied that moving a family of six would not be easy, especially because we had just settled in Kelowna the year prior. He added that he'd consider one, though, once he knew the details. "I'll take that as a yes," Dodd answered.

The prospect of running LMPL, a company of about 1,000 employees, piqued Paul's interest. While there was no job offer per se, it did seem logical that Radler would want Paul in the presidency. There was a real void of senior leadership at the company because Rick O'Connor, LMPL's vice-president responsible for the publications, and the Madison partners had left the company. Dodd was a financial executive, who also had duties with their other papers. He was clearly out of his element running LMPL. Paul, on the other hand, had spent more than 20 years running multiple publications. No other publisher in the chain had that experience.

We discussed what we might do if a job offer materialized. We decided we could continue to live in Kelowna, with Paul flying to the head office in Vancouver on Sunday nights and back home on Thursday nights. It was only an hour-long flight each way. He would spend Fridays working out of the Kelowna office. It all seemed rather exciting.

In the weeks following the January meeting in Vancouver, several things had Paul scratching his head. Hollinger's head office cancelled previously approved technical equipment without explanation. He then heard rumours about a new owner for the competing Thomson-owned Daily Courier. Thomson Corporation wanted out of the newspaper business and had sold off most of its assets. The Daily Courier and Penticton Herald were orphans with few potential buyers, especially with their history of labour problems and economic struggles. Several months earlier, David Black had decided to abandon his purchase of the troubled Daily Courier. At the time, we did not know why, but would several years later read about the circumstances.

We heard that Todd Vogt, a 32-year-old protégé of David Radler and a former senior executive in the Hollinger organization, might buy The Daily Courier. When Paul called Dodd and confronted him with the rumour of Vogt's ownership, Dodd said, "I understand that to be true." Paul then asked if this wouldn't be a contravention of competition law, because it was widely assumed that Vogt was still working for Radler. Dodd responded ominously, "This is beneath their radar."

Then a light bulb went off in Paul's head. But now, Paul thought, might Radler try to buy The Daily Courier for Hollinger and try to engineer a rationalization of the Kelowna newspaper market? Paul figured

Radler knew that common ownership of both papers in a market would open the door for exponential profits by repositioning the products, thereby reducing direct competition. There was one big problem, however: the federal Competition Bureau would likely prohibit a common owner of both papers in one market. The Competition Bureau, as an independent law enforcement agency, ensures that Canadian businesses and consumers prosper in a competitive and innovative marketplace.

From that point on, Paul took copious notes of everything that transpired.

Paul called Dodd again to find out more and was told, "The daily is always the dominant product." Paul disagreed, citing Cambridge and Guelph as two Ontario cities in which he had competed and where the free paper already was, or was in the process of becoming, the dominant newspaper.

Paul advised Dodd that he was concerned about his employees, assuming the plan was to marginalize the Capital News. Dodd bristled, responding, "There are two things you need to be concerned with: one is your company and other is your career."

During this time, Paul often spoke with Brin, the publisher of the Southam/Hollinger-owned daily in Kamloops. Brin had a great sense of humour, which helped us cope with our increasingly disturbing situation. To our young daughter's delight, Brin also reserved us tickets to the Shania Twain concert at the Kamloops arena in April 1999. During intermission, we met up with him and another newspaper publisher, Bob McKenzie, who worked for Hollinger. They and Paul started talking shop and, of course, Paul brought up the subject of Vogt and his Hollinger connection. "I've been told no good will come of talking about what's going on in Kelowna," McKenzie warned.

On May 1, 1999, it was announced that a new company called Horizon Operations had acquired The Daily Courier, Penticton Herald, and their joint publication called Okanagan Saturday, as well as 33 U.S.-based newspapers. What wasn't announced was that all of the U.S. titles had been bought from Hollinger. Vogt, Horizon's reputed owner and president, suggested to the community through interviews and his newspaper column that he was independent of his former company and of its principals, Conrad Black and David Radler.

Barely in his thirties and retaining a boyish look, Vogt had worked for Hollinger in both Canada and the U.S. He had held various high-level positions reporting directly to Radler. He was just what his boss wanted: someone who was bold and aggressive and would do exactly what he was told. In his newspaper columns, Vogt wrote unabashedly about his independence and even closed each column with "Todd Vogt owns the daily newspapers in the Okanagan." He gave interviews to business and trade magazines emphasizing that he was no longer associated with Hollinger and giving the clear impression he was *the* owner of Horizon. Those of us in the business, however, knew otherwise. He was more of a figurehead who was not far from his former bosses, the same bosses who owned the Capital News.

In a story published on page A3 of the Daily Courier's Okanagan Saturday on May 22, 1999, reporter Ron Seymour wrote about the new boss, saying Vogt looked more like a newspaper boy than a newspaper owner. At 32, he could pass for 22. To paraphrase Seymour, the article said that Vogt came across as friendly and approachable, and that generally everyone on staff seemed to like him and admire how much he had accomplished. The article also stated that just a few months prior to purchasing The Daily Courier, the Penticton Herald and the Okanagan Saturday from Thomson Newspapers, Vogt had been vice-president of Hollinger International. "Based in Chicago, he (Vogt) oversaw the day-to-day operations of dozens of small and mid-sized American papers."

Vogt had also been the communications director for the Social Credit Party in B.C., where he was born and raised. It was when he was working as the development director for the Vancouver Symphony Orchestra that David Radler offered him a job. The interview between Seymour and Vogt reveals that Vogt had virtually no publishing background at that time, having briefly held a job as advertising manager of a small newspaper in Terrace, B.C. "Considering my age, I don't think there's any other company that would have given me that kind of experience," Vogt is quoted as saying. He was also entrusted by Radler to run Radler's own private business interests, ranging from motels to jewelry stores.

Near the end of the article, Seymour mentioned that Vogt was the point man when Hollinger sold off scores of its smaller U.S. newspapers. According to Seymour, Vogt went to Radler in December 1998, and told Radler he'd like to buy some of the papers himself. The article states:

> *His mentor (Radler) was agreeable – but (Vogt's) wife (Colleen) took some convincing. 'When I told her we were going to go $50 million in debt to buy some newspapers, she got worried and asked if we'd have to take a second mortgage on the house.'*

The article reveals that as the owner of Horizon Publications, Vogt had papers across the U.S., including Florida and Hawaii, generating annual revenues of about $65 million. Vogt told Seymour that he had moved quickly to buy Thomson's Okanagan papers in Penticton and Kelowna when he heard plans to sell their Okanagan newspapers to B.C. newspaper publisher David Black had fallen through. He said he could have stayed in Chicago and run the papers from there, but he thought it was important to set up Horizon's headquarters in the Okanagan so he could be "close" to his biggest papers.

Paul perceived Vogt as a driven person, with a massive ego and a willingness to do whatever Radler commanded. Paul remembers the late John Collison, former LMPL president, telling him that Vogt couldn't utter a sentence without mentioning Radler's name.

Vogt had an extroverted personality and wrote glowing columns in The Daily Courier, ingratiating himself with the community. However, there was another side to him. His management style caused hard feelings among his employees, some of whom we knew.

Prior to the advent of the Internet, newspapers were by far the most dominant of all media. The highly competitive newspaper business surpassed radio and television in both news content and advertising revenue. In addition, many people considered print media to be the most trustworthy source of news. To protect their franchises, daily newspaper owners in many North American markets developed shoppers, publications consisting exclusively of advertisements. Like a bottom feeder, shoppers would soak up surplus advertising dollars to hold at bay competition, such as free circulation community newspapers.

So Paul, as well as many of his colleagues, thought Radler was trying to sneak Vogt in as an independent owner, to avoid scrutiny from the Competition Bureau. Paul thought he smelled a rat and figured that Radler would gradually turn the Capital News back into a shopper, allowing the daily to prosper without a direct competitor. That would explain the hiring freeze and Dodd's insistence on a shopper product in Vernon. Paul thought this fit Radler's modus operandi: own smaller daily papers in non-competitive markets.

Paul's blood was boiling. "I believed if this scheme came to fruition, the editorial content of the Capital News would most certainly be gutted."

Meanwhile, he and his management team had visions of putting The Daily Courier out of business and owning the newspaper market. In that scenario, Hollinger shareholders would be the biggest winners. In June 1999, about a month after the Horizon announcement, Paul was summoned to Vancouver for a meeting with Dodd at his office. It was Paul's first visit to the low-profile headquarters of Hollinger in Western Canada and the site of Radler's main office.

"Dodd started the meeting off by telling me that Vogt was a kiss-ass who would do anything Radler asked. He then paused and said, 'I guess you could call me a kiss-ass, too.' Dodd explained to me that I could be very useful in helping them make a lot of money in the Okanagan. He told me that Vogt may need to take a strike, and asked me, 'Would you be willing to print him?' Then he asked me if I had a good distribution manager."

The idea of helping someone you're trying to put out of business would otherwise be unheard of, but they were now one company – at least that's what Paul was told. Dodd explained that Horizon had been set up by Hollinger to buy back newspapers in the States that Hollinger had previously sold to non-publishing companies such as pension funds. Businesses such as those didn't know how to maintain newspaper profits and wanted out, but it wouldn't look good selling them back for less than they paid, especially to the company who originally sold them. This turned out to be a lie, but it was a plausible reason for Horizon's creation and explained why they didn't want its ownership made public. Paul clearly saw their motive in the Okanagan was to avoid Competition Bureau scrutiny.

Dodd asked if Paul had phoned Vogt. Dodd had asked him to do so several weeks ago. Paul said he had not. To Paul's surprise, Dodd said, "I think that's the right approach for now."

Paul told Dodd that if their plan was to marginalize his operations, he wanted a buy-out. Dodd did not respond. Dodd ended the meeting by telling Paul to be "unemotional," and, "Lie low; I had to do that once." Finally, he enjoined Paul, "Enjoy your family and go skiing in the Okanagan."

Playing games and dodging the truth are the antitheses of Paul's straightforward, no-bull approach. He had suspicions his company might be breaking competition law and he could only infer from Dodd's "lie low" comment that they wanted him to play along. Paul had been pumped about competing head-to-head with The Daily Courier when he first signed his contract. He now suspected, though, he was working for a company that owned both the daily and the community papers. That was the case where he worked in Ontario, but it was open and legal. With Hollinger in Kelowna, Paul was being asked to keep the ownership of the competing daily a secret, to keep it "under the radar" of the Competition Bureau.

VI

WALKING A TIGHTROPE

"Our lives begin to end the day we remain silent about things that matter." - Martin Luther King, Jr.

Paul, who was in his mid-forties when we lived in Kelowna, had developed a reputation as a fair-minded boss, who had a special talent for seeing the whole picture. His budgeting and analytical skills were extraordinary and many, quite mistakenly, saw him as someone who cared only about numbers and profits. In reality, he cared deeply for his employees, considering them family. He was a disciplinarian, true; if you screwed up, he wanted you to admit it and learn from it. It was only if your philosophies and values did not benefit the whole, or if you lied to him, that Paul had no qualms about firing you.

In Kelowna, he desperately wanted to protect his own family, as well as his staff and all of their families, from the damaging effects of Radler's scheme. He remembered all too well the point in his career when his corporate owner, Southam Newspapers, shut down the printing press operations at Fairway and many of his employees lost their jobs as a result.

"It was political gamesmanship with our big corporate owner. I knew it was wrong to shut down my printing press in favour of another one in the corporation. I wanted the decision to be reversed, but I was told the script had been written and not to worry about my own position. It turned out to be a disaster. I was outraged. I should have put my job on the line then."

Now here he was, some years later, with a different company in a different city basically being told the same thing: don't worry, you're a valuable executive. Dodd had advised Paul to "lie low" in the summer of 1999 and not to concern himself with Vogt, a man Dodd considered a "kiss-ass." During their June 25 meeting in Vancouver, Paul asked Dodd if there was any news on the Penticton Western, a Sun Media weekly Paul wanted in his stable. Paul reminded Dodd that Radler had called Sun Media president Paul Godfrey back in November. Radler left Godfrey a message, requesting it be added to a list of newspapers Hollinger wanted to buy from Sun Media. Dodd said he hadn't heard anything and suggested calling Bill Dempsey, the chief operating officer at Sun Media, to inquire about the acquisition of that Penticton paper.

Paul knew Dempsey from his Ontario days. He called him, and they had a short conversation in which Dempsey told Paul that he couldn't say anything about the Penticton purchase, but to talk to Dodd. Dempsey finished by rather mysteriously saying, "The horses will cross the finish line." Paul did then call Dodd, and explained that he felt he was getting a run-around. Dodd said he couldn't say anything and then confronted Paul with, "I hear you've been talking about Todd (Vogt)."

Paul had been walking a tightrope since he had been told not to say anything about the president of Horizon Publications, and specifically not to say anything about the young, private newspaper owner's connection to Hollinger. At the same time, he wanted to be forthright and to put the cards on the table. He felt strongly his bosses wanted to turn the Capital News into a shopper, which would have been bad for the newspaper, its readers, advertisers and especially its employees. He wanted to stop that from happening. Paul acknowledged to Dodd that he wasn't hiding facts that Vogt had already revealed, especially the $8-million loan he secured from Hollinger to help finance his original Horizon acquisitions.

Just days before Paul's conversation with Dodd, Vogt had announced that he was launching a new daily newspaper in Vernon. This seemed fishy to Paul. No one had started a local daily newspaper in decades.

Paul asked Dodd for further clarity on what Hollinger or Radler or both were up to.

Dodd answered, "The less you know, the better; the less you say, the better. You're part of a large corporation. Accept it." He also told Paul that, at some point, they might go for a walk around the block and he'd fill him in but, if later questioned, would deny having done so. Paul remembers thinking that this was starting to seem like the way the Mafia operated.

He figured his employees would soon be sacrificed, even though the Capital News was profitable and The Daily Courier was not. He was extremely anxious. On one hand, Paul was under the impression he was about to be promoted; on the other hand, he was being told to keep his mouth shut and help his competitor.

The summer of '99 brought with it ongoing skirmishes with Vogt as he attempted to disrupt Paul's operations in various ways. Vogt planted rumours that he would soon be buying the Capital News. Vogt also started contacting Capital News employees. He asked Alan Monk, the Capital News manager responsible for its healthy, weekly real estate publication, and two other managers about moving to The Daily Courier. Monk had strong relationships with local realtors and likely could have moved advertising from the Capital News' Real Estate Weekly to the Courier's similar product, Home Finder. There's an expression in the newspaper business: "Ads go where ads are." The Capital News clearly owned the real estate advertising market in Kelowna, and Vogt was trying to steal a key employee to gain traction for his product. Of course, there was nothing wrong with that. It happens all the time in business. However, Monk told Paul that Vogt had gone to some length to explain there was no connection between the two companies.

Monk declined Vogt's offer. It certainly seemed hypocritical and arrogant when Vogt, the 'independent' and competing paper's owner, countered with, "How long do you think it will be before I play the Radler card?" Vogt also approached Gary Johnston, Paul's Vernon publisher. He asked him rhetorically, "How long do you think David Radler will support your money-losing paper?" He suggested to Johnston that he might have an opening for a publisher at his Penticton Herald daily paper. Johnston didn't bolt, but his senior reporter, Russ Niles, did, accepting the role of editor of Vogt's short-lived Vernon daily.

LMPL'S chief financial officer, Orest Smysnuik, told Paul that Dodd had told him that "Vogt was on a leash" and that Dodd understood it was Radler holding it. Rumours abounded. The games continued over the summer and into September. Capital News editor Andrew Hanon got a call from Universal Newspaper Syndicate asking him to confirm something. The woman told Hanon that Todd Vogt called her and said both Kelowna papers had a common owner. Vogt told her there'd been a mix-up and the Roger Ebert column should be directed to The Daily Courier and away from the Capital News. Hanon instructed her not to move the column and immediately spoke to Paul, who called Dodd. Dodd was agitated because he had no control over Vogt. His suggestion to Paul was to retaliate and "cancel an order of newsprint on Todd." Paul was taken aback. Dodd was suggesting that he pose as Vogt, or one of his senior executives, and cancel a load of paper. He also remembers Dodd remarking, "Todd is a very nasty young man."

Other than ramping up the competition, Paul couldn't do much to stop the chicanery. Angus Reid had conducted a follow-up readership survey in March 1999 and the results showed that the Capital News had exponential gains in all areas and had clearly beaten The Daily Courier in every area of comparison. Since the re-launch of the paper in 1997, advertising market share had grown from 33 per cent to more than 50 per cent.

"The Angus Reid employee we dealt with said she had never seen such a dramatic increase in readership and wondered if the survey methodology had been changed from the original survey in 1997. It hadn't. The results showed that the Capital News was now regarded as the number one source of information for the community, surpassing all other media," Paul declares.

He and his ad team got over 30 advertisers to provide testimonials about how great the Capital News was. These ads were backed up with charts using the Angus Reid data, clearly illustrating that the Capital News was a better buy for advertisers in the Kelowna market.

Paul says, "I did the opposite of helping my competitor, and launched a massive testimonial ad campaign underlining the benefits of our paper compared to his. We were tops in overall readership, classified advertising, real estate advertising, and flyer distribution."

The Capital News also published a four-page wrap around the paper announcing the survey results. *"The results are in again and it's time to say Thanks. We're proud to say you're reading a winner."* The promotional brag sheet showed the Capital News in the leading position in the crowded media market. *"The gap between us and our competition is larger than ever,"* crowed the copy. Fully 77.5 per cent of the adults in Kelowna/Westbank were reading the Capital News each week. Westbank, then unincorporated, is now part of the District of West Kelowna.

Paul was having fun as the Capital News publisher, more fun than at any other time in his newspaper career. However, the publisher's position was not part of the employment contract when LMPL hired him. He wouldn't have moved west just to be publisher. Even the general manager's job was a very "thin" position by industry standards, as there were only six papers in the group.

He had agreed initially to be the interim publisher of the Capital News when former publisher Jim Clark exited in February 1997. That three-month timeframe had stretched into a year. In a memo dated March 23, 1998, to Rick O'Connor, vice-president of LMPL and Paul's boss at the time, Paul wrote:

When Jim Clark resigned, I was told to hire a publisher to replace him. A few months later that changed and the company informed me that they would like me to assume that responsibility. Let me be clear, I am not unhappy or disgruntled. On the contrary, I have quite enjoyed most aspects of what I am doing professionally, especially the role of publisher of the Capital News and overseer of the related printing and distribution businesses. That said, this position is not the one I was appointed to perform. I came here to be General Manager of a group of six newspapers and make several strategic acquisitions that would allow us to be the dominant newspaper operation in the Okanagan. To date, that has not worked out.

Meanwhile, after my rocky first-year adjustment as the general manager's wife, I had gained more confidence personally and professionally. I was involved in community initiatives and doing freelance writing and radio reporting. As Paul had advised when we first moved to Kelowna, I did get, on my own merits, some reporting work at the Capital News. I wrote a variety of news/lifestyle and entertainment feature stories for the weekend papers. Around mid-1999, I became the contributing editor of the Family section pullout, in the Sunday edition of the paper. I had free creative reign and covered a broad range of topics and issues. I often focused on local families and family life. My beat ranged from the serious to the humorous. My slice-of-life column, A Parent's View, developed quite a following over two years. The Family section was well read and I received many letters to the editor. I was passionate about my section, as indeed I have always been passionate about family life and its importance to society as a whole. I took full ownership and accountability. It was my lifeline and connection to the community. I had found my niche.

Paul was now struggling to find his.

VII

A PURE NUISANCE

"Rumor travels faster, but it don't stay put as long as truth."
- Will Rogers

A definite highlight of 1999 was returning to see family in Ontario that summer. We stayed at Paquana Cottages, my family's traditional vacation spot on Muskoka's Lake Rosseau. There, we reconnected with friends and enjoyed a brief reprieve from the newspaper business. Paul had pre-arranged to have surgery at St. Joseph's Hospital in Toronto during that vacation. Throughout his life, he had suffered from extreme sweating in his hands and feet and he also flushed and blushed easily. Our doctor in Kelowna diagnosed him with a rare condition called hyperhidrosis, a malfunction of the sympathetic nervous system that causes considerable embarrassment and emotional stress in sufferers.

Paul had previously been advised against the somewhat risky and rather complex surgery that could alleviate the symptoms and was told to continue to live with it. He did a Google search and discovered that a Swedish surgeon had pioneered a safe endoscopic method to surgically clamp the offending nerve located at the back of the chest cavity. When Paul read that late one night, he woke me up and announced he was going to Sweden.

Luckily, though, he found out a doctor in Toronto had learned the technique. Contact was made, tests completed and surgery booked. The operation was a success. Instantly, there were no more sweaty hands and there was a marked improvement in the other symptoms. Unfortunately,

Paul has had to live with the common post-surgery compensatory sweating that results in excessive sweating from his torso when his body temperature is raised. My finely-tuned sweating machine!

Returning to B.C. we were, of course, buoyed by the outstanding survey results that showed the Capital News as the leader in the crowded Kelowna media market. In November, we celebrated 15 years of marriage. Despite this, my "Mary Lynn vibes" sensed looming misfortune. I'm not an astrologist, but it felt like our stars were misaligned, set on some sort of cosmic collision course, high in the sky above us.

Indeed, business just kept on getting more and more bizarre – and entertaining – as the year progressed. It all seemed surreal. The long-time Thomson-owned Daily Courier now had an owner who was a former Hollinger International senior executive. Vogt, the owner/publisher, wrote some outlandish statements in his newspaper column. Those made us cringe in horror and laugh at the same time. "He's pretending to be an independent owner and he's misleading the people of Kelowna," I remember Paul saying.

In late September, Paul wrote a letter to Dodd, though ultimately he decided to discuss it with Dodd in person instead. He had written:

> Todd Vogt's 'acquisition' of The Daily Courier continues to cause concern, confusion and frustration among our managers and many of our staff. It seems obvious to our management team that our parent company is attempting to marginalize our business in favour of the Courier. Regardless of what is said concerning Todd being independent, the evidence is to the contrary. Our managers remember David Radler's visit last October when he pledged the support of the corporation's national-account (advertising) reps to the Capital News. Now that Todd has the Courier, those national-account reps are officially repping him and not us.

In early October, while Paul was driving Dodd and Orest Smysniuk, LMPL's VP of Finance, to the Kelowna airport, Dodd again raised the suggestion of Paul printing The Daily Courier in the event of a strike or lockout. He asked Paul to "think outside the box." What he said next truly infuriated my normally calm and steady husband. He asked if Paul could set up a press in a barn.

"I couldn't believe my ears!" Paul recalls. "A paper like ours prays for the day when the local daily is unable to publish over a labour dispute. And here I was being asked to arrange to have a newspaper press set up in some out-of-the-way location so my competitor could get printed."

Paul's face must have betrayed his reaction, because Dodd sternly delivered his next line: "Be unemotional. I can assure you Conrad Black and David Radler are unemotional about business decisions."

Paul snapped back with, "That's easy to say. It's not them or their staff who are being affected." Dodd warned Paul that Radler was coming to Kelowna the following week and advised Paul not to get upset about anything Radler might say to him.

As predicted, Paul got a call on October 13 from Radler. "Paul, it's David Radler. I'm at the enemy's. I'd like to bring Todd over with me to your building. How do you feel about that?" Paul advised him that it wasn't a good idea to bring Vogt over from The Daily Courier because there had been rumours circulating for a few months that Vogt was poised to purchase the Capital News. Anxiety was running high in Paul's staff.

Radler replied, "OK then, but you'll have to take us to the airport once we're finished." Outside Paul's office, Vogt dropped off Radler and Jack Ferguson, the VP of manufacturing for Hollinger. Radler and Ferguson each had copies of Vogt's Daily Courier tucked under their arms. They came into the conference room and Radler asked Paul, "Have you been watching what I've been doing?" He was wondering if Paul was aware of his recent acquisitions.

Paul wanted to embarrass Vogt, so he told Radler about Vogt acknowledging common ownership in Kelowna to the Universal Syndicate representative as a means of moving the Roger Ebert column out of the Capital News and into the Courier. Radler didn't bite. He sloughed it off by saying that Vogt knew Ebert from his Chicago days and that Paul was being too hard on his young competitor.

Radler then got to the purpose of his visit. "He explained what he termed 'Hollinger's approach' to a labour problem: The unions were the enemy and helping any publisher, friend or foe, is what we do. He said we would be printing Vogt's papers if he had a labour disruption. He finished by saying, 'We'd even print for David Black, and he's not a good guy and Todd is.'"

Paul tried to keep his cool. He was being asked to do something that was clearly not in the best interests of his operation, and possibly a breach of competition law.

Certainly Paul knew of non-union publishers printing for papers in strike situations, but he had never heard of doing so for a direct competitor. After all, a disruption would be a major competitive advantage for the non-union paper. Historically, the Capital News profited during the daily's strikes; it was how it had gained dominance in classified advertising and flyer distribution.

Paul told Radler that his paper had improved profits by a million dollars since Radler's visit less than a year before. Radler's response was, "Yeah, but it's not three or four." Paul's Kelowna operation was now making about $2 million per year and The Daily Courier was likely losing a bit. If a common owner could reposition the papers and avoid as much direct competition, three or four million in profits could easily be realized between the two entities.

Paul asked Radler if he could cite any examples where a direct competitor printed a rival's paper. He remembers Radler giving him some obscure response that didn't make sense.

The main reason Ferguson was with Radler on this trip was likely Hollinger's upcoming launch of the National Post. The irony of the labour-disruption talk was that it was The Daily Courier's press that was being considered to print the Post, not Hollinger's Capital News press.

Almost two weeks later, on October 25, Dodd called Paul to discuss some day-to-day matters. Dodd eventually said that Paul had achieved his maximum bonus for the year. He added, "Mr. Winkler, we need to talk about your career." He acknowledged that things hadn't worked out as Paul had intended. Paul could only agree saying that yes, his reasons for making this move had evaporated. Dodd explained that Paul was competing in an artificial environment. He wanted to get together in mid-November because he was going to be away for a couple of weeks. Dodd suggested he might have something to offer Paul in Vancouver. Otherwise, he encouraged Paul to call Bob Calvert or Michael Sifton, the executives who ran Hollinger's Canadian non-metro dailies. Paul had no interest in leaving or being pushed out of Kelowna, so he didn't make any call.

By November, the walls seemed to be closing in and emotions were running high. The stars had begun to collide; the tension in the air was palpable. Still, we were surprised when Paul received a voice mail from David Black, president of Black Press, owner of dozens of Western Canadian and some U.S. papers. David Black, no relation to Conrad, competed directly with Hollinger in many markets.

"I'm not sure what David's intent was, but his message was rather chilling and caused me concern," Paul admits. The message, which follows, started off with a referral to a phone call Paul had had with his former boss, Rick O'Connor, now group publisher for David Black. During that conversation, Paul had shared his suspicions and concerns about what Radler was up to in Kelowna. The message was:

Paul, David Black calling. I was at a do last night with Rick O'Connor and he and I were talking about your phone call and starting to worry a little bit that you are getting yourself and everybody there, everybody's getting themselves into untenable positions and somebody could accuse people of collusion I guess, and I don't know how you defend yourself against that. If you know for a fact that the other paper's owned by the same people and you haven't said anything, it seems to me you're kind of guilty by association even though you had no part in it. So I just wanted to chat about it with you. Does sound a little worrisome and if you want to talk to me ...."

He then left Paul several contact numbers.

Paul didn't call him back, but the message prompted him to seek legal advice from Vancouver law firm Harris and Co. He wanted to ensure that he and his managers were not in breach of any laws.

Paul had been successful in avoiding face-to-face confrontations with Vogt. Unfortunately, at the beginning of November, we ran into him at a Central Okanagan Foundation (COF) dinner event. Paul was set to announce to the group the establishment of the Kelowna Capital News' Millennium Fund. At that time, I was the local Millennium project coordinator. Ours was one of many community foundations participating in this national program encouraging individuals and groups to mark the millennium in a meaningful way by undertaking a special project. The local foundation set up a registry where people could detail their projects and be recognized. The Capital News announced its project, the establishment of a Millennium Fund, with the COF. The paper had commissioned local artist Alex Fong to do a painting for the cover of the Capital News millennium magazine. Numbered prints by Fong would be sold, with proceeds going to the fund.

Paul, philanthropic by nature, stood up to announce this initiative. Immediately after, to our great surprise, Vogt stood, too, to make his own announcement about a Daily Courier donation to the COF. It seemed he was deliberately upstaging the Capital News.

On November 2, Dodd called Paul and said things were happening in the company and that he wanted to meet with Paul as soon as possible. Was this about Vogt buying the Capital News? We had heard yet more gossip about Vogt wanting to acquire it. The next day, Paul found out that Frank Tesky had resigned. Tesky was a well-regarded publisher who ran some of LMPL's Vancouver-area papers. Paul then wondered if they were going to try to push him into that job, in a desperate attempt to get him out of Kelowna.

Paul flew to Vancouver two days later, on November 4, to meet Dodd in his office. Paul, who now had legal advice, took charge of the conversation. He said he wanted answers about what Radler was up to in Kelowna.

He further said that if there was a common owner, and if it was legal, he wanted to run the combined Kelowna operations. Then Dodd drew three circles, two side by side and one above. Paul wondered what the circles meant, but Dodd never elaborated. All he said was it wouldn't be possible for Paul to run both and it wasn't because of Vogt.

Paul pressed forward, telling Dodd he had sought legal advice based on his contract and that without clarity over their plans and a timeline for him to assume the job he had been hired to do, the company was in breach of his contract. Dodd said he didn't know anything about Paul's contract but that if it had come to that, Paul should send him a copy. The meeting ended with Dodd shaking Paul's hand and saying, "It's so unfortunate, Paul, we worked so well together. You're just too pure."

Paul had dinner with Orest Symsniuk that evening in Vancouver. He shared with the LMPL vice-president of finance what had happened at the meeting with Dodd. Paul said that he figured his time in Kelowna would soon be coming to an end. Paul was sad it had come to this but he also felt a sense of relief that the untenable position he'd been put in would soon be over. Symsniuk said he would pass a copy of Paul's contract to Dodd.

What else was Paul to do? He had been hired for a particular role. The 1996 contract from LMPL specified the job description for general manager of the Okanagan group of newspapers. Two years later, the papers were fully owned by Hollinger. It was obvious to Paul that both his role and the company's direction had changed. Carving out a new role in the company would only drag him deeper into what he reckoned might be fraudulent activity. He had no interest in that.

He wondered if he should claim constructive dismissal. This is a common legal action for situations where the employer has not directly fired the employee but instead has failed, in a major way, to comply with the employment contract. If the employer has unilaterally changed the terms of employment, the employee is more or less forced to quit.

Paul knew that his superiors wanted him out of Kelowna because he wasn't co-operating with them. Moreover, he didn't want to work for them anywhere else or in any other capacity, having learned what type of operators they were. He and his lawyer drafted a letter. They were cautious not to allege any wrongdoing by anyone because Paul couldn't prove anything. He simply wanted out of a situation where he no longer felt he could lead with integrity.

Paul faxed this letter, labelled "personal and confidential," to Dodd on November 17, 1999.

Dear David:

As we have discussed, David, my purpose for having moved to Kelowna has failed to materialize for a variety of reasons well beyond my control. As I have repeated to you, I am not interested in continuing to be the temporary publisher of the Capital News, or assuming any other role, without the assurance that I will be assigned the general manager's position and original mandate that I was promised within a specified period of time in the near future. You have now confirmed that this will not happen.

With that in mind, I would like to commence severance arrangements with you. I have contacted the Vancouver legal firm of Harris & Co. to give me advice on this matter. Their review of my circumstances confirms that I have a clear case for constructive dismissal. I have also been advised that I have a case for negligent misrepresentation against the Company based on the representations that were made to me with respect to my position and which never materialized.

Pursuant to my employment contract, I am entitled to 12 months' pay in lieu of notice. In addition, under the circumstances, I am advised that I am entitled to further compensation for damages that I have incurred as a result of my move from Kitchener to Kelowna. I therefore propose to settle my claim against Lower Mainland Publishing on the following terms:

1.   I will continue in my current position until Jan. 3, 2000. As I have 14 days of holidays remaining, I will stop reporting to work on Dec. 10, 1999, although I will continue to be paid until Jan. 3, 2000.

2. I will receive in the normal course of events, the bonus I am owed for the period of Sept. 1, 1999 to Dec. 31, 1999 in the amount of $10,611.

The letter then outlined the terms regarding paying Paul out with one year's salary and benefits, the costs associated with moving back to Kitchener, and his legal fees. It continued:

I would expect the Company would comply with any reasonable requests concerning the payment of the above in the most efficient manner permissible by law.

I am deeply saddened that events have turned out as they have, but I must remain true to my beliefs and principles. I must also keep the well-being of my family in mind.

David, I understand your frustration with my need for clarity, reasonable control and independence over what I am responsible for. I also believe you do have some understanding of where I am coming from.

I look forward to hearing from you before Nov. 26. Please call me if you wish to discuss things.

That same day, Vogt was at a Chamber of Commerce dinner. In his ongoing rumour campaign, he approached Maxine DeHart. This well-known local businesswoman was also a Capital News freelance columnist. She called Paul the next day to say that Vogt asked her if she had heard "the rumour." Vogt didn't expand and left his comment dangling.

Paul didn't know how to respond to DeHart. Was Vogt's "rumour" comment to DeHart on the very day Paul had sent his letter to Dodd a mere coincidence, or just part of Vogt's ongoing campaign to inform people of his purchase intentions of the Capital News? Maybe his vague comment was just happenstance. However, the bizarre event that happened the next morning convinced us the letter's contents must have been leaked.

VIII

THE FRIDAY OF THE LONG KNIVES

"The melancholy days are come, the saddest of the year,
Of wailing winds, and naked woods,
And meadows brown and sear." - William Cullen Bryant

Thursday, November 18, 1999. It's all so vivid. Paul was munching on a morning bagel from his stash in the lunchroom freezer at the Capital News. He was listening to the Daybreak morning show on the local CBC radio station. The host, Alison Paine, was doing reaction interviews to a controversial news feature the Capital News had published the day before about a charity fundraising event for Big Brothers. The paper's attention-grabbing headline, *Gentlemen's Dinner labelled a "Pig-fest,"* caused quite the stir in the community.

The paper had reported on an Okanagan Valley event that hundreds of prominent businessmen had attended. There was a lot of drinking, cigar smoking, and even young women modelling lingerie, at what had been billed as a Men's Night Out. Our undercover reporter filed his story for our Wednesday edition. It created quite a flap for those attending – and for their spouses.

"The representatives of Big Brothers were clearly upset with our coverage and I was listening to their reactions on Daybreak when Karen Hill, our business manager, stuck her head in my office around 9 a.m. She said, 'Oh, you're listening to the radio,' in quite a serious tone," Paul remembers.

When she realized he was listening to another local station, not SILK FM, she told Paul what had been broadcast on SILK. They had reported that the Capital News had been sold to Todd Vogt and that Paul Winkler was gone.

"If our paper's been sold, no one told me," he responded.

Paul was incredulous. He called up the station and told them that he was not gone; he was, in fact, sitting in his office chair. Furious that no one from the station had called him to verify the facts, he demanded to know where they got such information.

They apologized profusely and pointed to a blog by freelance writer Brian Lightburn. Lightburn had written: "This column has just received information that would indicate that The Daily Courier has purchased the Capital News, pending Southam Board approval. The publisher of the Capital News, Paul Winkler, has apparently resigned."

SILK retracted its story throughout newscasts that day, but the damage had been done. The radio announcement that Paul had resigned was unnerving, to say the least, and it spread like wildfire. I heard about it through the grapevine. When I arrived to work at the Central Okanagan Foundation office that morning, its executive director, Janice Henry, told me in a very concerned voice about a message she had just received. The COF board president, Alan Dolman, had heard the report and called her immediately. The news hit me like a ton of bricks. Stunned, shocked, my brain whirled. I felt dizzy and sick.

While my stomach was in knots, Paul seemed calm because he knew what was coming. I couldn't get my head around this strange turn of events. I could not face reality. I could not, would not, endure more turmoil because we deserved better. We had jumped over hurdles to finish the race and I had finally caught my breath. I almost convinced myself that the radio announcement was a bad joke, a prank committed by a schoolyard bully. I willed myself to believe that everything would work out.

Paul phoned Dodd and left him a message, but Dodd didn't get back to him regarding the radio report. Paul remembers being in the Capital

News lobby at around two o'clock when the receptionist interrupted his conversation. She told him, in a surprised but urgent voice, that Todd Vogt was on the line and wanted to speak to him.

"I dashed upstairs to my office. It would be the first time Vogt and I chatted on the phone. He said he wanted to meet me for coffee right away. I said there was no way I would meet with him and that too many people were connecting our companies. I told him about the message from David Black suggesting collusion between our two companies and that I had no intention of getting together."

Paul thinks that call was one last attempt to get him onside with their plans.

Having spurned Vogt, he got a call later that afternoon from Dodd, who left a message on Paul's voicemail: "Mr. Winkler, I will be in Kelowna tomorrow to have a meeting with you, sir, between 3:15 and 3:30. If you'd like, you can call me at home tonight."

As Paul left the office around 5 p.m., Alan Monk, the real estate ad manager, stopped him. He told Paul that some of his clients were claiming to know the lawyers who were doing the deal for the Courier to buy the Capital News.

Paul did call Dodd that evening from our home, just before six o'clock. "I told David I thought I knew where this was going. I asked if we could chat." Assuming the following day would be his last, Paul wanted to talk things out to ensure a smooth transition. Dodd was not in the mood for chatting and said, "No. It's gone too far." At the end of this very brief call, Paul suggested they not have the Friday afternoon meeting at the Capital News building. A retirement party would be taking place there for Ray Higgs, a much-loved real estate advertising rep.

He and Dodd decided to meet at a local restaurant.

After that phone call, Paul and I went out for a dinner we had booked a while earlier with his friend Dale Brin, the publisher of the Kamloops Daily News. He told Brin that he anticipated being fired the next day. Brin thought Paul was overreacting and that Hollinger would come to its senses.

Twelve hours later, in the midst of our normal morning routine, as Paul pulled on his socks, he asked me what the date was. I thought it odd, but told him.

"November 19th," he echoed. He sat still for a few seconds, then turned and met my gaze. "It's the date my dad died."

Paul rarely speaks about this anniversary because his father died in 1961, when Paul was only eight years old. "I'm going to get fired today," he then added bluntly and without emotion.

He was so sure that Friday was to be his last day that he packed up his office belongings in a box that he put in his car prior to meeting Dodd. At the restaurant, Dodd showed Paul the announcement he was going to post at the Capital News. Paul remembers feeling it was surreal, reading this:

David Dodd, President of Lower Mainland Publishing, regrets to advise all staff that Paul Winkler, Publisher of the Kelowna Capital News and General Manager for Lower Mainland in the Okanagan, has advised me that he is severing his employment with us.

Paul has been the Publisher of the Kelowna Capital News since November 1996 and has made a great contribution to the activities of Lower Mainland in the Okanagan. Since I became President of Lower Mainland approximately one year ago, Paul and I have enjoyed a very productive relationship. I very much regret this recent development in our relationship, as I believe that we have made some significant, positive steps over the last year.

I am pleased to advise you that Richard Sadick has accepted the appointment of interim Publisher and will take up his responsibilities on Monday, November 22, 1999.

Paul wryly noticed that Dodd made a factual error in the announcement. Paul had not been publisher since November 1996; he became publisher in the spring of 1997.

Dodd then handed him a letter in an envelope, which Paul did not open. "I asked him if he wanted my keys and he said I was welcome back at the office to attend the retirement party if I wanted to."

Paul of course declined and they parted ways. Only when Paul got into the car did he read what Dodd had handed to him:

November 19, 1999

Dear Paul,

I write in reply to your letter of November 17, 1999, in which you advise that you have sought legal advice and wish to commence severance arrangements with your employer.

I do not agree that you have been constructively dismissed. I have made no changes to the terms and conditions of your employment. You state in your letter that "I am not interested in continuing to be the temporary publisher of the Capital News, or assuming any other role, without the assurance that I will be assigned the general manager's position and original mandate promised within a specified period of time in the near future." Further, you allege that I "confirmed" that the above would not happen. I have no knowledge of your assertion that you are the "temporary publisher" and I at no time confirmed that any of the above would or would not happen.

However, as you advise that you are severing your employment, I accept your resignation.

David Dodd

Paul sat behind the wheel, dumbfounded. "I remember saying to myself, 'They've left me high and dry. Fired without severance and saying I'd resigned.' In the best-case scenario, I thought my letter claiming constructive dismissal would have prompted Radler to abandon his Horizon plan, whatever it was exactly. My worst-case scenario was that he wouldn't change his plan, but that they would pay out my contract just to get rid of me. I should have known Radler wouldn't have been swayed and that paying me out could be viewed as admission of some possible guilt. I'm sure he knew I wouldn't sign a gag order in exchange for a payout."

They cleverly tried turning Paul's constructive-dismissal letter into one of resignation, giving them the means to get rid of him. In retrospect, Paul doesn't think he could have handled the situation differently. He was not prepared to compromise his principles.

Paul didn't get to say good-bye to his employees, many of whom had become like family. Because he had already packed up his belongings in anticipation of "The Boot," he came home immediately after the meeting. When Dodd returned to the Capital News, he spoke with the management team. Moreover, he passed out Paul's "confidential" letter, with the numbers blacked out, and told them he couldn't comprehend why Paul would write such a letter. Alan Monk, one of the managers, remembers many of the Capital News employees walking around in "kind of daze and denial, the same kind of thing that hits you when you receive traumatic news."

Editor Andrew Hanon coined it "the Friday of the Long Knives."

I was at the kitchen sink, oblivious to all of this, when I heard the side door open. I turned and saw my husband standing in our back foyer, among the pile of kids' coats and shoes. He had a small box under his arm, and his face looked woeful, yet stunned. My heart sank. I cried out "Nooooooo!" before he even uttered a word.

IX

A CAGED TIGER

"Never give up on something that you can't go a day without thinking about." - Winston Churchill

Despite all the fears of computer meltdown and dire predictions from the doomsday faction, the new millennium came and went without incident. Nothing crashed except my husband's job and our dreams. I thought surely we would wake up from this nightmare; it must just be a very bad dream. Paul's bosses would admit the error of their ways, reconsider, and see things the right way: Paul's way. But, of course, we had to face reality. Paul warned me not to get my hopes up that his bosses would offer compensation. So, rather than wallow in self-pity, we developed a number of strategies to safeguard ourselves against depression and to be good role models for our children. We drew on our faith and spirituality, for one.

We were active and regular churchgoers in Kelowna. We were members at St. Charles Garnier parish, pastored by Father Gord Walker, an affable priest. He reminded us of one of the players on the Flying Fathers, an old-time hockey team of Roman Catholic priests. Paul is not Catholic, so we also often went to Trinity Baptist Church, a large congregation led by Pastor Tim Schroeder, a dynamic and eloquent orator. The Sunday following Paul's firing, I was the scheduled reader at St. Charles. While practicing the passage I had to deliver, Paul and I were awed by how strongly the message applied to our situation. The timeliness and hopefulness of the words from Ezekiel, chapter 34, verse 15-17 touched us deeply.

I myself will be the shepherd of my sheep, and I will make them lie down, says the Lord God. I will seek the lost, and I will bring back the strayed, and I will bind up the injured, and I will strengthen the weak, but the fat and the strong I will destroy. I will feed my sheep with justice. As for you, my flock, thus says the Lord God: I shall judge between one sheep and another, between the rams and the goats.

We knew that we had to hang on to our faith for the wild ride ahead. This was reinforced when Paul told his mother in Kitchener about my reading and relayed how the words had buoyed us. Coincidently, she read the very same Ezekiel passage in her daily devotional book the day after that call! She cut it out and mailed it to us. We kept rereading those words and they truly helped us make a horrible situation constructive rather than destructive. We elected to become better, not bitter.

Paul describes getting fired as being a bit like attending his own funeral. He says, "There were so many people who contacted me in the following days, offering their condolences and words of encouragement. There were also a number of people I thought I'd hear from but did not, especially within the LMPL family." He wondered if the other publishers, who were based in the Vancouver area, felt some animosity toward him because so many of them had applied for the position that he, an outsider from Ontario, had secured.

Still, a small group of people who had access to inside information at Hollinger kept Paul informed about what was going on. In this book, some of those sources will go unnamed, but their valuable insights were recorded in Paul's 300 dated and diarized notes chronicling phone calls and meetings from early 1999 to early 2002.

Although his departure caught some off guard, many suspected it was connected to the shenanigans with Todd Vogt and The Daily Courier. All Paul knew for sure was that Radler was trying to hide any connection he, Conrad Black and Hollinger had with Vogt's Horizon. Paul was sure they were in breach of Canada's competition law, but he was not yet aware that they personally owned Horizon. At the time, he believed that

Hollinger controlled Horizon and used it, as Dodd had earlier explained, as an arm's-length business to buy back papers in the U.S. that Hollinger had previously sold to pension funds. Those pension funds, Paul had been told, didn't know how to maintain profits, and were willing to sell those papers back at a loss, but it wouldn't look good if they were sold back to the company from which they were purchased.

Meanwhile, despite the extreme awkwardness of the situation, I continued to freelance for the Capital News. I remember sneaking up the back staircase to the newsroom to fetch the staff camera on the Monday after Paul's firing. I wanted to avoid my colleagues, for fear I would break down. I particularly did not want to see Richard Sadick, Dodd's interim publisher. Sadick had, from that day on, switched his loyalties from Paul to Hollinger. Prior to Paul's firing, Sadick seemed at least as upset as Paul was with what was going on. That appeared to change the instant he became publisher and was reporting to Dodd.

I managed to slip over to the filing cabinet in the conference room, unnoticed. However, when I retrieved the camera, my movement caught the eye of a colleague, the arts and entertainment editor, Jean Russell. When our eyes met from her nearby cubicle, I burst into tears. She came to me, embraced me, and didn't say a word. I so appreciated her empathy and quiet support.

Our world had been turned upside down and I willed myself to stay positive and not to worry. Paul had never been unemployed in his life. He hadn't stopped working full-time since he started in his late teens. Heck, thanks to my quick deliveries, he didn't even take a full day off when our kids were born. Unemployment was very different and far more challenging than he would ever have expected. I remember coming home from work or from doing errands and he would be staring out the sliding door to the backyard patio, holding his bifocals in his hand, twirling them in tiny circles over and over again. I told him he looked like a caged tiger.

When Paul sets goals, he is relentless about achieving them, and this proved to be another great strategy to help us through the crisis. His first goal was to find a job. "There were six mouths to feed," he explains. "Mary

Lynn was working about 20 hours a week at relatively low pay. Our oldest, Patrick, had just turned 13 and our youngest, Jake, was six. Finding a job wouldn't be easy, given that Hollinger controlled so much of the newspaper industry in Canada. I was a specialist at running chains of community papers, so finding the right opportunity would be difficult."

His second goal was to try to negotiate a settlement with his former employer. He returned to Harris & Co., the Vancouver legal firm who drafted his infamous – some said "hard-edged" – letter claiming constructive dismissal. Paul had many personal and professional contacts within Hollinger and Southam, which Hollinger had bought out. Paul hoped to connect with these former associates.

If all else failed, he knew he would have to take legal action. This would be our absolute last recourse, because he knew it would likely be a protracted and expensive process. "Few people have sued Hollinger, Radler or Black. In fact, it's usually them doing the suing. I wasn't aware of too many cases where Radler or Black had lost a legal battle," Paul points out.

His third goal was to expose what Radler and, by extension, Conrad Black and Hollinger were up to with Horizon. The biggest media company in Canada, and the third largest newspaper company in the world, was engaged in what Paul believed was a scam.

His fourth and final goal was to thwart what clearly appeared to be Radler's plan for Kelowna, thereby saving jobs at the Capital News, especially in the newsroom. Again, it was well understood in the newspaper industry that optimal profits and protection from other print competition could be achieved with a local daily and a shopper under common ownership. Paul remained sure this was what Radler had in mind, and it would require turning the Capital News back into the shopper publication it once had been. The Competition Bureau never stood in the way of common ownership of a local daily and a shopper, but often objected when two competing newspapers were brought under common control. Paul reasoned Radler wanted to sneak this by the federal government and gradually trim the news content in the Capital News.

For several weeks prior to and shortly after Paul's departure, Vogt seemed to want to tell as many people as possible about his company, Horizon, buying the Capital News. Paul didn't see the purpose, other than to seek attention – something Vogt seemed obsessed with in his weekly columns – and to possibly disrupt the Capital News staff.

The day following Paul's firing, Vogt wrote a column touting the "success" of his new Vernon daily paper, claiming it was Canada's fastest growing newspaper. He ended the column with this paragraph:

As I said, we are in the North, Central and South Okanagan and we have every intention of staying. To add credence to this commitment and to continue turning the rumour mill, not only do we plan on staying, we have firm plans in place to expand in the not to (sic) distant future. I wouldn't want to leave any of you with nothing to talk about."

The fact that the Vernon paper ended up being published for only six months before he shut it down now makes us laugh at his pontificating.

But the expansion Vogt hinted at with his readers, combined with his outright statements to others, meant only one thing to Paul: Radler intended to have his publicly traded company, Hollinger, sell its Okanagan papers to Horizon, a company Paul knew Radler had control over but whose ownership remained a mystery. Despite Vogt's prolific pronouncements, the purchase of the Capital News had not yet been consummated. Perhaps Paul's somewhat public departure had caused them to delay it in the hope that the dust would settle and not attract the attention of the Competition Bureau. Perhaps the Competition Bureau was already involved, maybe tipped off by competitor David Black of Black Press, who published the Vernon Morning Star.

There is little doubt that the deal was supposed to have happened. Vogt testified a few months later, at a B.C. Labour Board hearing, that he was attempting to buy Hollinger's Capital News and the Vernon Sun Review, but received a phone call saying that would not be possible.

By this point in time, the Capital News managers and some staff were apprehensive about their futures. Various sources told Paul that Horizon's Daily Courier was getting special treatment from Hollinger's national advertising sales representatives. They had included The Daily Courier in presentations to major clients and left out the Hollinger-owned Capital News. Likewise, Hollinger/Southam began running help-wanted display ads in The Daily Courier, dropping the Capital News and depriving it of that revenue.

Back in the fall of 1999, before Paul was let go, he found out that Hollinger had established an Income Trust that included all of the papers in his parent company, LMPL. He then found out that his group of Okanagan papers was not included in the trust. He asked at that time why the papers he managed had been left out and received a nonsensical answer from Dodd. A veil of dishonesty, mistrust, doubt, deception and trickery hung heavily over us, as well as over our Capital News colleagues and friends. It was a veil Paul had long wanted to rip apart, if only he could. He felt powerless and frustrated. Industry insiders told him they had seen documents showing links between Hollinger and Horizon. Paul wanted copies so he would have tangible proof of what everyone in the business believed to be true: Vogt was nothing but a frontman for Radler.

We received support from a handful of friends and family, even from some of Paul's former employees. If there were any doubts that Paul had had a great rapport with his staff at the Capital News, they were put to rest at the paper's annual Christmas party, the month following his departure. On November 30, Sadick called to say that the staff had overwhelmingly voted Paul Employee of the Year. He invited us to the staff-run Christmas party. Management had never been eligible for the award and though Paul wasn't management anymore, neither was he staff. He figured they wanted to present him the award for standing up to Radler. It turned out that wasn't the reason, because many staff members were confused about his departure and Dodd's spin on his departure. Staff simply wanted to honour his contribution to the business. "Receiving that award was one of the proudest moments of my life," Paul remarks.

The evening was bittersweet. It was bitter because Paul had been unceremoniously dumped by the owners, yet sweet because his former staff acknowledged his commitment and competence. What a great testament to his character and leadership skills. Staff members gave Paul a painting and some of the nomination comments were read aloud. "I know managers are exempt," one nominator wrote, "but since he is no longer with us, I truly believe he should be honoured by the staff and company he served in such an exemplary, caring, professional manner. No one, including any past publisher in my time (28 years) has done such a fine job. I really hope this nomination will be seriously considered."

Another nominator wrote, "Because he is brilliant … yet warm and kind and humble and fun… and he's led the Capital News through some of the most positive changes ever!"

They cited him as being a great leader, with a sense of humour, who always had time to listen. "Paul was very involved in the interests and needs of the Capital News staff. He initiated and improved benefits, profit sharing and started paid sick days. A team spirit in the building was revived that was noticeably missing. I feel Paul brought the Capital News into the '90s and new millennium with both the treatment of the staff and the look and content of the paper."

Soon after the party, we got word of two recognitions the paper had received under Paul's tenure. One was completely unexpected. It came from the LMPL family of publications, recognizing the Capital News as its top newspaper. "That was quite an honour in and of itself, but even more special because it topped the North Shore News and Vancouver Courier, who had placed first and second respectively in all of Canada the previous year," Paul said.

We weren't as surprised when the Capital News received an award for its millennium magazine, which was distributed on January 1, 2000, from the association of Suburban Newspapers of America. The glossy, colourful news magazine, with the front-cover artwork by Kelowna's Alex Fong, took first place in the SNA's special section category. The project, spearheaded by Paul, was near and dear to me as well, because I had decided to see what it was like to be an advertising rep and I sold some ads for the publication.

After it sunk in that Hollinger considered Paul's constructive-dismissal claim as a resignation, Paul wrote Dodd. On December 1, Paul outlined his thoughts about what Hollinger's actions meant. He explained to Dodd what happened immediately after they parted ways.

> *I did not open the letter until after our meeting and was surprised that you claimed that I had resigned. I never intended to, and did not resign. Since that time, on November 29, 1999, your lawyer has written to my lawyer indicating that he has instructions to accept service. I understand this to be an invitation to me to sue you.*

> *I implore you to reconsider your position and meet with me to find a mutually beneficial way of sorting all of this out.*

Silence. There was no response from Dodd at all. It could mean only one thing: Hollinger did indeed expect Paul to go through the lengthy and costly process of suing them.

Paul remembers that a couple of weeks after his firing, he met with LMPL's VP of Finance, Orest Symsniuk, who flew in from Vancouver to go over annual management bonuses for Paul's direct reports. Symsniuk said to Paul, "Dodd has no ill feelings toward you and said you were the best strategic publisher he'd worked with." At about the same time, Paul had also heard from another source that Hollinger "will drag their legal claim out as long as possible," and warning that Paul "should not expect any offer to settle."

On December 13, Paul got a call from Paul Feurer, a regulator with the Competition Bureau. Grateful, Paul thought that reinforcements had come to our aid. He gave Feurer an overview of what had happened, as well as the names of several of his managers who had pertinent information concerning links between Hollinger and Horizon.

A few days later, he received a call from Duff Jamison, the successful operator of a chain of community newspapers and printing operations in St. Albert, Alberta. Jamison's business was partially owned by Hollinger/Southam, so he had had dealings with Dodd. As a friend, Jamison attempted to help Paul get a settlement so we wouldn't have to go to court. He said that he spoke with Dodd for about 45 minutes and that Dodd had confirmed two things. First, just months prior to getting "The Boot," Paul was going be asked to head up LMPL, now a wholly-owned subsidiary of Hollinger with about 1,000 employees. Second, Hollinger was not interested in mediation to settle Paul's claim and he had better be prepared to take them all the way to court.

In early January 2000, Paul spoke with David Black to follow up on job opportunities. In that conversation, David Black told Paul he didn't buy The Daily Courier back in 1998 when he had announced his intentions because he had checked with the Competition Bureau to see if he could secure the Capital News as well. The Competition Bureau told Black that he could not own both papers. Paul remembered Dodd telling him in the spring of 1999 that what Hollinger was doing in Kelowna with Vogt was beneath the Competition Bureau's "radar." David Black had been up-front, whereas Radler's approach was don't ask, don't tell.

Vogt said no more about buying the Capital News and its sister, the Vernon Sun Review, but he did something that rocked the Capital News editorial team. Andrew Hanon, the editor at the time, called the incident "an unsettling fracas." It made the ties between the Capital News and The Daily Courier very clear. There had been a lot of press about the murder trial of Shannon Murrin, accused of murdering eight-year-old Mindy Tran in Kelowna. Murrin was acquitted. Following the sensational conclusion of the trial in Vancouver, both Hollinger's National Post and Vancouver Sun managed to get exclusive photographs of him leaving the Vancouver courthouse. The Capital News had worked closely with the Vancouver Sun to cover the story. Their union was a competitive advantage over The Daily Courier because the Capital News and the Sun were affiliated through Southam Newspapers, which Hollinger owned at the time. The Sun was prepared to share the photo with just one newspaper: the Capital News. However, Vogt's Daily Courier got the photo as well.

The Daily Courier management told the furious Capital News staff that as Canadian Press members, The Daily Courier was entitled to the photograph, too. However, the Capital News editorial staff got wind The Daily Courier was granted the photos after Vogt and Radler became personally involved to ensure their paper got the photo at the same time.

Thanks to the efforts of Andrew Hanon, Capital News editor, I maintained my freelance work putting together the Sunday Family section. I was writing in a vacuum, making as few trips to the Capital News building as possible. It was cathartic to stay on to write and connect with my readers. Maintaining a positive and optimistic outlook, I managed to not come across as being too desperate in my slice-of-life columns. I only infrequently mentioned my unemployed husband, our children's stay-at-home dad. Fortunately, I wrote under my maiden name, McCauley, and did not tell my readers where Paul had worked or about the circumstances surrounding his job loss. I did subtly hint about it by writing columns on the topic of the importance of integrity and telling the truth. Less than a month after that awful Friday in November, I wrote about how our family dynamics had changed now that my husband, who used to work at least 50 hours a week, was at home all day. It was so strange, I mused. At his insistence, we had cancelled our cleaning lady's services. In my column, I bemoaned the fact that despite his good intentions, it was difficult to teach him domestic skills and routines. I relayed how impressed I was that he had cleaned bathrooms once, but how the residual Ajax fumes had almost made me faint. After opening the windows, I remarked to him how heavy-handed he was with the cleaner. Flummoxed, he replied, "Well, if you're going to do a job, you have to do it right."

I'm sure that publishing my work drove freshly minted publisher Richard Sadick crazy. I never did find out what Dodd thought about me writing. I'm not even sure he knew who I was, although I'm sure

Sadick filled him in. In a January 2000 column, I wrote another light-hearted piece providing an update about how a formerly busy executive was making the transition to stay-at-home dad.

It's been well over a month since my husband has been unemployed and just about all my hopes and dreams of turning him into Mr. Domestic have evaporated. 'You mean he isn't running around the house in an apron with a feather duster in his hand?' a publisher colleague joked with me.

I went on to say that despite Paul's need to stay busy, I still couldn't convince him that he should help me out more with the laundry and house-cleaning. I told my readers how difficult it was to share my "space" with him and that he was always underfoot. I admitted that I felt totally vindicated, though, when I heard him say how relieved he was when our four children returned to school after the Christmas holidays. "I love them dearly," Paul had said, "but you sure can't get much done when they're around."

I also informed my readers that Paul did, however, take over grocery shopping and cooking duties during our role adjustments. I have to admit that his budgeting and money sense made him a food shopper extraordinaire. After hockey, saving was his favourite sport. And, oh, how he gloated when he came in under budget.

On several occasions, the cashiers told him they were surprised that his bill for the overflowing groceries in his cart wasn't higher. At that time, we were watching every penny. The secret to Paul's success was a spreadsheet of dinner menus with the items he needed divided into "Really need" or "Buy only if a really good deal." He used this as a guide while scanning the grocery store flyers. He shopped at three or four food establishments to stock up on the best deals.

As a columnist, you have to guess who is most likely to read your stories. I imagined my audience to be similar to my neighbours. I was hopeful that they liked my self-effacing humour and would pick up on my sincerity. I never wanted to talk over my readers' heads nor did I simply want to repeat what they already knew about families. I wanted to build on their knowledge. Every journalist is hopeful that he or she has a "following," but one never knows. When people acknowledge or react to your stories through letters to the editor or phone calls, you are truly grateful.

I wrote about three columns describing Paul's situation, knowing how sensitive a subject it was at the Capital News. There's an underlying feeling that even though you're not naming names or giving specifics, people know who you are and who your subjects are. I was therefore caught off guard when a woman heard me introduce myself to someone else and approached to ask, "Are you the poor reporter who has an unemployed husband?"

Paul and I had a good laugh about that afterwards. It's vital to keep your sense of humour through trying times. Thankfully, Paul could also have a good chuckle with his friend, Dale Brin, then the publisher of the Hollinger-owned Kamloops Daily News. I used to think Brin missed his calling as a stand-up comedian. Paul used to fax Vogt's column to him every Monday morning. Later in the day, they would debrief and chuckle over the phone about some of the absurd and egotistical things Vogt wrote. I was just grateful that I could still write at the paper. My job kept me grounded and kept our hopes alive that Paul, too, would once again work in his beloved industry.

My tiger escaped his cage in January, to go clear across the country to Newfoundland. Derek Hiscock, then the president of Robinson Blackmore Printing and Publishing, called not long after Paul was fired. Paul, who knew Hiscock through their mutual involvement in provincial and national newspaper associations, thought Hiscock was phoning because he had heard what had happened. Hiscock had not heard. He was calling to talk to Paul about Peter Kapyrka, The Daily Courier publisher Vogt had let go several months earlier. Hiscock was searching for an executive to head up his newspaper division at Robinson-Blackmore, based in St. John's. Kapyrka was a candidate.

Paul remembers the conversation quickly turned to whether Paul might be interested in running this group of about 15 papers across Newfoundland. Paul suggested that Hiscock hire him as a consultant for two weeks. That would give both parties an opportunity to go for a "test drive" before either committed.

Kapyrka and his wife, Cheryl, were eager to move back to the East coast, where they had family connections. Hiscock called Kapyrka to let him know that Paul was now his top choice for the job. Paul was a more likely candidate for this job – managing group operations for community newspapers – than was Kapyrka, a daily newspaper operator. It probably helped that Paul knew Hiscock personally. Kapyrka graciously offered to provide Paul the files he had received during his earlier contacts with Robinson-Blackmore. Paul really didn't know Kapyrka beyond the fact that he was the publisher of the Capital News' competing paper. Kapyrka's generosity, and our common bond of extreme suspicions of Vogt, launched a friendship between all of us.

Paul had never been to "The Rock," and he found it to be almost as beautiful as B.C. The warm weather that year further elevated his opinion. Newfoundland had one of its warmest mid-January temperatures ever recorded. One day while Paul was there, it was warmer in St. John's than in some spots in Florida. The famous East coast hospitality wowed him even more. He recalls his first day:

"I was surprised to be invited to a big party of Robinson-Blackmore employees at the home of the company's vice-president. I don't remember the reason for the party, but they made me feel like it was thrown in my honour. Everyone was so warm and welcoming and laughter filled the air. I remember the host's wife offering me an appetizer, and with a provocative twinkle in her eye, asking, 'Can I offer you some tongue?'"

This was cod tongue, a Newfoundland delicacy.

Paul was busy gathering information on the company for a report he would eventually write, so the two weeks passed quickly. On his way back to Kelowna, he stopped in Ontario to talk to key contacts in Toronto and to visit our parents and siblings in Kitchener-Waterloo.

Upon his return home, Paul wrote the report for Hiscock and sent it to him. Soon after, Hiscock offered him a job. I wanted to move from one end of the country to the other, from the sunniest to one of the foggiest regions, but Paul didn't want to commit immediately. He was hopeful two things might happen – something in Ontario would open up, or the Competition Bureau would act and force the sale of the Capital News to another owner, who would hire Paul back. He also had a nagging concern about Harry Steele. Steele was the founder of Newfoundland Capital, the transportation and communications company that owned Robinson-Blackmore, and he sat on the Hollinger board of directors. What would happen, Paul wondered, if we all moved out there and Steele made a deal with Hollinger! It never did happen, but it wasn't beyond the realm of possibility. Even Hiscock told Paul that it was possible. Ultimately, Paul declined the job offer and Kapyrka accepted it. Now it was Paul's turn to hand over the paperwork to our new friend.

Exercise and healthy eating were two other essential coping strategies. During the late 1960s, when he was 16, Paul ran 32 miles in a popular fundraiser called Miles for Millions. He was hooked, despite his brothers having to pull him out of the bathtub afterward because all of his muscles had seized up. He developed the habit of running not only to keep his heart healthy, but to purge workday stresses and tensions. Running seemed to keep his spirits up during this very tough experience. He decided he would train for the 2000 Okanagan Marathon, a little more than 30 years after his Miles for Millions run. This time, he would be prepared.

I was thankful that he had this physical outlet. However, my imagination got the better of me and I became frightened while he was running. Paul told me he felt like he had been working for the Mafia and because he had crossed Radler and was no longer a member of "the family," they had cut him off. One of Paul's newspaper colleagues said in jest that he better be careful a vehicle didn't "accidentally" hit him on the back roads. I may have overreacted, but this was an unusually unsettling time.

Spring in the Okanagan is truly rapturous. For Ontarians, who expect the season to be an almost indiscernible, sloppy extension of winter, spring in southern B.C. is blissful. During this season of growth, new beginnings and fresh starts, Paul finally received some hard evidence linking Hollinger and Horizon. In early March 2000, one month after his return from Newfoundland, Paul got a call informing him that a U.S. securities filing by Hollinger formally linked Hollinger and Horizon. It's called a 10 Q report. Paul's source faxed him a copy. In almost ineligibly small print, under the heading "Dispositions," it read:

During the second quarter of 1999, the Company entered into an agreement with Horizon Publications Inc. to sell 33 U.S. community newspapers for $43.7 million. Horizon Publications Inc. is managed by former Community Group executives and owned by current and former Hollinger International executives.

Unfortunately, no specifics were forthcoming. No names were mentioned, let alone how much each executive owned.

Paul understood that both Radler and Black personally owned a "big chunk" of Horizon. If this were true, the whole cover-up would go far beyond an issue with the Competition Bureau. It would likely involve securities law or even fraud. In other words, if Radler and Black privately and personally bought newspapers that were competing with their publicly owned newspapers, they could be in a conflict of interest and presumably breaching their fiduciary responsibilities.

If this were true, Paul thought, Radler and Black were playing with fire. That did not make sense. Why would these highly intelligent and supremely successful businesspeople involve themselves in anything that could potentially tear them down? Taking that risk, courting danger, in small-town Kelowna? It just didn't add up. Paul was surprised and confused by their seemingly cavalier corporate behaviour, but it spurred him on in his mission to seek the truth.

Paul then got word that Horizon was legally registered in New Brunswick. He pondered that. "Is it a coincidence that the Capital News company had also recently been registered there, too?" He passed this information along to an investigative reporter who was experienced in corporate searches. The reporter, Russ Niles, confirmed that both papers were registered in N.B. and were using the same legal firm. Both papers had Radler's Vancouver office listed as their "in-province" address.

Niles had been the top journalist at LMPL's Vernon Sun Review until Vogt hired him to be editor at his upstart daily in that same North Okanagan community. The Vernon Times was the much-heralded Vogt daily that lasted about six months, and Niles' tenure there was even briefer. He had watched Vogt in action and was almost as eager to expose the scam as Paul was. Niles was able to shed light on Paul's firing and how it was likely leaked to the local radio station before it actually transpired.

While working for Vogt, Niles was in The Daily Courier office on November 17, 1999. "I had bought a new camera in Kelowna to replace one which had been stolen," Niles recalls. "I went to the Courier to use their computers to finish off some work for the Vernon Times. Vogt was in his office and I took the opportunity to point out how many ads were appearing in the Friday edition."

Niles recounted to Paul that Vogt congratulated him and the Vernon Times staff on the fine job they were doing. Vogt said he intended to write his column about the Vernon daily's strong showing. Vogt also said that his proposal to buy the Sun Review and Capital News had been approved in principle by his bankers and would be going before Hollinger's board of directors on December 5. Vogt told him about Paul's letter to David Dodd and said that Capital News publisher Paul Winkler was being let go.

Niles remembers returning to the Courier's newsroom, where about three staff members quizzed him about the takeover plans. He told them what Vogt had said. He assumed Paul had already been let go, which of course was not the case.

Paul thinks that one of the Courier staff members, or Vogt himself, leaked the information to Brian Lightburn, who then wrote about it on his news blog, from which SILK, the local radio station, picked it up and broadcast it as fact the day before Dodd dismissed Paul.

Niles said Vogt was planning on buying the Capital News and the Vernon Sun Review and turning them both into shoppers. In other words, the plan was to get rid of the news content in the Capital News and thereby all but eliminate direct competition between Paul's Hollinger papers and Vogt's Horizon dailies. This was precisely what Paul had suspected.

Paul was increasingly concerned about the newsroom staff of nine people and their families. If the paper were turned back into a shopper, their positions would be cut. This also troubled Capital News editor Andrew Hanon, who now harboured real concerns about his job security and his future reporting to Sadick, a man he considered a puppet publisher with whom he had a strained relationship.

Paul admired and respected Hanon. "He did an outstanding job establishing the Capital News as the top news source in Kelowna, ahead of the daily, TV station and five local radio stations, as the Angus Reid and City of Kelowna surveys had proven. At the time, he was the sole breadwinner for his wife and four young daughters and he had a lot riding on what was about to happen."

Hanon said that Sadick was using Dodd's name to intimidate him. Sadick knew Hanon had maintained a close relationship with Paul, and he repeated to Hanon a phrase Dodd had used: "Loose lips sink ships."

By late March, Niles and Paul had sufficient documentation to visit some key area politicians, as well as the print, radio and television media, to make them aware of the unscrupulous activity occurring right beneath their noses.

"We even showed our evidence to some businesspeople like the manager of Sears, the Capital News' biggest advertiser," Paul recalls. "We were hopeful they could help put pressure on the Competition Bureau to act and halt any possible merger of the two papers, which would undoubtedly result in diminished competition and the elimination of news in the Capital News."

With documentation in hand, Paul set out, sometimes accompanied by Niles, and visited Kelowna MLA John Weisbeck, mayor Walter Gray, and councillors Andre Blanleil (a high-profile local businessman and one of a handful of people who befriended Vogt), and Ron Cannan (now a Conservative MP). Paul went to see Senator Ross Fitzpatrick, who was a personal friend of then Prime Minister Jean Chrétien. It was well known that there was no love lost between Chrétien and Conrad Black.

"Whether these visits made any difference, I don't know. I just felt it was my duty to make people of influence aware that there was a scam taking place in Kelowna and that it involved some very powerful individuals," Paul reasons.

Niles told Paul that he dropped off their evidence with his friends at The Canadian Press in Vancouver. CP is a news-gathering co-operative organization funded by its members, primarily Canadian daily newspapers.

Niles said that his CP contacts were scared, and he doubted they would do anything with the strong, documented tip because Hollinger/Southam was CP's biggest contributor and financial backer. What would be the point in risking their jobs over a story out of Kelowna?

In April 2000, while Niles and Paul continued digging, Niles, on an unrelated matter, attended a British Columbia Labour Relations Board hearing in Vancouver because it involved Horizon. Some interesting testimony was put on record. It was at this hearing that Vogt admitted under oath that he had been negotiating to buy the Capital News and the Vernon Sun Review, but had received a phone call the end of January advising him that his efforts had been unsuccessful. Vogt produced cell phone records showing his cell phone was billed back to Hollinger. Keith Mitchell, a Vancouver-based lawyer, represented Vogt at that hearing. Mitchell was known to represent Radler, too. Paul also learned that spring that Radler owned not just one but two homes in Palm Desert, California. He wondered if Radler's second home there was the address that Vogt had claimed he owned in Palm Desert.

Paul was beyond being a man on a mission. He was obsessed. This injustice was all he could talk about, not just with his colleagues in the newspaper business, but with our family and friends. They listened politely, but many people advised him not to fight the big guys. "You can't win," was a common refrain. Even Alan Monk, one of Paul's managers who admired Paul's stubborn stand, thought the battle was pointless. In 2013, we received this email from him:

> I remember thinking and at times telling Paul that he was being a Quixotic type of person. It seemed to many of us that he was a knight in search of dragons, and so he was inventing these stories…. We didn't really understand what was going on. After 2000, it became much more clear how wrong it all really was … to me. I have to say, I am exasperated with how little people understand to this day.

Friends, colleagues and family wondered why Paul was getting so hot and bothered; that's the way business runs, they opined. Just before firing him, Dodd had said to Paul, "It's such a shame you're just too pure." Even Niles, Paul's partner in exposing what their former bosses were up to, said off-handedly that Paul would be crazy to leave the Okanagan and that he should go get a job at Radio Shack. I had to admit to Paul that I had nagging doubts and questioned whether he was onto something really big or was certifiably nuts. I knew I had to trust him explicitly, though, for our marriage and family to function. Without trust, fear would rule.

Paul wrote Dodd again, in an attempt to open communication with his former boss. Paul wanted to set the record straight on some idle gossip surrounding the reason for claiming constructive dismissal. Paul learned a rumour had been going around the Vancouver office where Radler and Dodd were working the week Paul sent his letter claiming constructive dismissal. The rumour was that Paul might replace John Baxter, who was about to retire as president of Metroland, Canada's largest newspaper company. There was no truth to it, but Paul reasoned that if Radler and Dodd heard it, it might have impacted their decision to fire him rather than pay out his severance. He tried to demonstrate a conciliatory tone in his letter, telling Dodd that rumour had been false. Paul didn't expect a reply, and didn't get one, but at least he could say he made an effort to dispel any misperception they might have had.

The bureaucratic wheels turned agonizingly slowly. Paul called his contact at the Competition Bureau again and was frustrated, but not surprised, to learn that the Bureau was still in information-gathering mode. He became increasingly impatient, sitting on the sidelines.

Hollinger's annual meeting was to take place on May 24, 2000 in Toronto, and Paul hatched a plan. He called his former competitor and adversary, Bob Verdun, a newspaper publisher from Elmira, Ontario, who in his retirement devoted much of his time to being an outspoken shareholder activist. A recipient of the Michener Award, Canada's highest journalism award, Verdun made headlines following the annual meetings of many of Canada's major publicly traded companies. He loved to challenge chief executives when shareholders and the media were in attendance.

Paul describes his plan. "I wanted to force Conrad Black and David Radler to talk about Horizon and what was going on. With this in mind, I called Verdun. After reviewing my material, he said he would bring it up at the annual meeting in May. Verdun told me he liked Black, though, and had lunched with him and Stockwell Day (a former Conservative MP and former leader of the Canadian Alliance Party), following a previous Hollinger annual meeting."

Anderson Charters, our friend and co-owner of Trajan publishing along with Paul Fiocca and Paul, was at the May 24 meeting, too. He recounted for Paul what was said. According to Charters, Verdun asked about ownership in Horizon. Conrad Black said that neither he nor Radler played an active role in Horizon. Black went on to say, as reported in The Globe and Mail the next day, "I own a few shares because they needed a balance of sale but I have nothing to do with it." Paul wondered what "a few" shares meant. We would learn much later that "a few" meant 24 per cent of the company – hardly insignificant.

Verdun asked Black what happened to Paul Winkler in Kelowna. Black deferred to Radler, who replied that Winkler was a disgruntled employee who had left the company.

We remained hopeful that Hollinger would settle Paul's claim of constructive dismissal and save us the misery and cost of going to court. However, comments from Paul's contacts made us recognize that that was a very unlikely scenario. Paul heard in December, "These guys will drag out Winkler's legal claim, and Radler goes 'ballistic' when he hears Paul's name mentioned." Paul also heard that Hollinger's national ad-sales division's sales reps had labelled him a troublemaker. In early spring, Paul called Tim Peters, Southam's vice-president of human resources, to ask his advice on how to resolve the fact he had been fired without severance. Peters offered to call Dodd, but acknowledged that Paul's only probable option would be going to court.

On April 4, 2000, in the glorious Okanagan spring, Paul wrote a four-page letter to Don Babick, then the president of the Hollinger-owned Southam Newspapers and the first publisher of the recently launched National Post. He had known Babick when Paul worked for Southam as president of Fairway and Brabant newspapers in Ontario. Babick reported directly to Conrad Black. Paul says he considered Babick a man of principle. He hoped that Babick, after reading about Radler's activities in Kelowna, would consider them serious enough to inform Conrad Black. "Maybe Black would take action," Paul remembers hoping. "At the very least, it put Babick, a senior executive, on notice of what I alleged had gone on." Neither Babick nor Black responded.

Faced with the very real possibility of going to court to win a settlement, Paul decided to change law firms. The big Vancouver law firm he was using was expensive and far away. He hired a Kelwona lawyer, Alf Kempf, who specialized in employment law with the firm Pushor Mitchell. Paul and Kempf became partners in May 2000 as Paul negotiated a partial contingency agreement. In layman terms, that meant Kempf would work for a reduced hourly fee and get a percentage of Paul's award, if victorious. Kempf proved to be very strategic and Paul came to the table with conviction he had the moral upper ground. I believed that together, he and Kempf were both "bigger" and smarter.

In anticipation of a court battle, that summer Paul contacted his former managers and asked them if they would write their stories about what had happened at the Capital News during the past year. Paul drafted some ideas and sent them the outline for them to edit, approve and sign. Not everyone had a story to tell and some of those who did, declined. Understandably, there was considerable fear of the unknown among them.

In one incident, the Capital News publisher, Richard Sadick, exacerbated this fear. Paul notes: "Real Estate Weekly manager Alan Monk told me Sadick confronted him when he heard I was trying to get these letters signed. He told Alan I had been blackballed in the industry because of my stand and that if Alan were to supply me with a letter, he would face similar treatment." Monk said he remembers hearing that anyone who supported Paul would be finished in the industry. He called Paul almost immediately after that incident and Monk, too, diarized it. He was indignant and thought it a blatant interference with justice.

X

AND, THE BUYER IS...?

"Our real blessings often appear to us in the shape of pains, losses and disappointments; but let us have patience and we soon shall see them in their proper figures." -Joseph Addison

What do you do when the primary breadwinner is no longer making money? We thought that selling our house would be a logical step to take. In the spring of 2000, we called our real estate agent Bud McGrath, who got all the particulars in order. Our kids were devastated. One morning, I noticed the For Sale sign missing from the front lawn. After quizzing everyone, our daughter finally confessed. She and her friends had hidden it. The only semi-enthusiast was Jake. He was six at the time and did love to play real estate agent and give guided tours of the house to prospective buyers. After four months of no real offers, in late summer, we took the house off the market and breathed a collective sigh of relief.

The dictionary defines "limbo" as a state of confinement or a place of oblivion, forgotten, cast aside or obsolete. I could use that metaphor to describe our situation, but it seems too weighty and depressing. Instead, I compared our situation to being stuck in a traffic jam. Limbo is nebulous; a traffic jam is real. I get cranky and impatient stuck on the road, unable to go forward or backward. My nerves become even more frayed in a car filled with kids. I am so jealous of those heading in the opposite direction, speeding by, seemingly getting to their destination with ease. I often look longingly at the paved shoulder of the road, restraining my desire to swerve over and peel away on that restricted zone. If Paul is driving, I sometimes ask him to get out and see what's going on. After scrutinizing the situation, he inevitably returns to the van to tell us he really doesn't know how long we'll be stuck.

At that point, you have no choice but to make the best of it. We play games such as I Spy with the kids, to occupy their minds. Instead of complaining, we focus on being grateful that our air conditioning and windows work. When we start to inch forward we're excited, and soon we're at the speed limit with a renewed appreciation for a smooth and steady ride.

The year 2000 was like a traffic jam. Paul and I enjoyed the points of acceleration along the way, then patiently inched forward, optimistic the jam would clear soon, so we could move toward our destination once again.

The days were exceptionally sunny and long. In June, there was a glimmer of hope for employment. David Black of Black Press and his right-hand man, Bob Grainger, contacted Paul and offered him the job of publisher of their Alberta operations. Those included some community papers and a daily, The Red Deer Advocate. Although Paul was not a fan of small daily papers, especially if they were up against a good community paper, he did know something about the Red Deer market. He and his Capital News editor, Andrew Hanon, had been there in February, consulting for Duff Jamison of St. Albert, David Black's competitor. Jamison had bought the struggling community paper in Red Deer.

Misgivings aside, Paul needed work and said he couldn't be too fussy. "Grainger and I talked about the job and everything looked pretty good on the surface," he recalls. "I had one big concern and that was whether David Black would do a deal to sell or trade his Alberta operations in exchange for a strategic asset of Hollinger's or Vogt's Horizon in British Columbia." In B.C., David Black was a significant player. His Alberta properties, though, were minimal. The Red Deer Advocate was the only daily David Black had in Canada, while Hollinger and Horizon owned many dailies in the surrounding area. So, if David Black did do a deal with either of those newspaper companies, Paul could find himself working for either Radler or Vogt. And needless to say, that would not be good!

"I told Grainger that I'd accept the job with the understanding I'd receive a two-year severance if Hollinger or Vogt's Horizon, or any of the individuals linked to those businesses, acquired the Advocate. The last thing I wanted was to move my family of six again and find that per- haps, soon after, I might be reporting to the same people I'm suing."

Grainger said Paul's request was a bit unusual, but he didn't think it would be a problem. Black Press offered to have the entire family visit Red Deer to check out housing and visit the paper. Knowing the kids weren't keen on leaving Kelowna, we tried to make the potential move appealing. We made arrangements to take them by train and to stay at the West Edmonton Mall Hotel, in one of its very large theme rooms.

Unfortunately, the day before we left for our Alberta adventure, Grainger told Paul that David Black would not agree to the two-year severance demand. We couldn't really cancel our reservations, so we went ahead with the trip. Paul thought it a futile endeavour. I didn't care anything about futility. I so badly wanted Paul to get a job, I tried to send telepathic vibes to David Black to re-negotiate with my husband. Off we went, so Paul could meet with the Advocate's departing publisher, Don Moores.

Days later, when we returned home train-lagged, Paul received a letter from Grainger, saying he and David Black wanted to hire Paul and build toward a long-term relationship and more responsibility down the road. Without that severance guarantee, though, Paul still had to tell them he could not accept the position. The only tangible thing that came to pass from that trip was a column for me: "Rockin' and Rollin' Through the Rockies on VIA Rail."

As summer's heat and holidays gave way to autumn's cool breezes and the start of school, we shored up our energy. Paul in particular kept physically fit and mentally sharp to brace himself for every eventuality.

They say what is expected is never as overwhelming or frightening as the unknown. However, we were up against a company whose operators kept everyone guessing.

Paul's lawyer, Alf Kempf, suggested that instead of preparing for a full trial, he and Paul would first try using Rule 18A, also known as a summary trial. This is a trial using documents only, in this case to establish whether Paul's letter claiming constructive dismissal was a letter of resignation. Each side appeared before the judge to argue whether to proceed with this. Paul says, "Hollinger argued against it, I'm sure because all they wanted to do was drag this whole process out, hoping I'd wave a white flag of surrender. I didn't attend the hearing, but the judge ruled that a summary trial would not be possible. This left me no choice but to proceed with a full trial or give up, and giving up wasn't in the cards."

We continued to wait with bated breath to see what Hollinger would do with the Capital News. We hadn't been officially notified, but it was pretty clear, after that much time had elapsed, that the Competition Bureau had nixed Radler's plan to consolidate the newspapers in Kelowna under a common owner.

The question that remained was who would end up owning the Capital News. Paul heard that it might be sold to CanWest, a Winnipeg-based media company started by Izzy Asper, owner of Global TV network. This made sense to Paul because CanWest had bought most of Hollinger's papers earlier in the year as part of a $2-billion deal. Paul was sure the Competition Bureau would want to examine this deal because CanWest owned the Kelowna TV station. This news briefly lifted Paul's spirits as he pondered the possibility of being hired by CanWest to run a combined TV station and local paper. That possibility was quickly dashed. He heard the CanWest deal was off. He later confirmed it was indeed because the Bureau would not approve it.

After months of serious physical and mental training, the marathon race Paul had been gearing up for arrived. On the Thanksgiving Day weekend, about one week before his 47th birthday, he completed the

Okanagan Marathon in a very respectful three hours and 50 minutes. The kids and I volunteered to help at the water stations and we were so, so proud of him. When he crossed the finish line, we gave him a group hug and took his picture with his medal. With this major accomplishment under his belt, Paul felt reinvigorated and more than ready to handle the turbulence ahead.

It arrived more quickly than we anticipated. Like a scene out of a B-Grade horror movie, the phone rang many times on October 24. The caller, whose voice I did not recognize, seemed demanding. He wanted to speak to Paul, who was out working as a consultant for one of Kelowna's largest Internet service providers. We didn't have call display, so I asked the caller if he wanted to leave a message. He refused. He called about four times, sounding more agitated each time that Paul had not yet returned. He absolutely would not leave a message.

When Paul finally arrived home, I quickly told him about the numerous, unnerving phone calls. He checked the call history and discovered the number originated from The Daily Courier. Who could it be and why? We both jumped when the phone beside us rang at that instant. Paul answered. The caller was Todd Vogt. I became alarmed when I heard Vogt yelling through the receiver at my husband.

He had called to say he was very upset with Paul for bad-mouthing him around town and that Paul had better stop. Paul asked him for details. Vogt said his friend told him that Paul had said terrible things about him. Again Paul asked for specifics. Vogt said he had been told he shouldn't go into a dark alley with Paul. However angry Paul might get, threatening or roughing someone up in a dark alley is so far from his style, under any other circumstance it would have been laughable.

Paul says, "Todd went on to dispute what I'd likely told his friend, that Todd's head office was also Radler's office. But I had the papers to prove that. Vogt also said I'd bad-mouthed him to his paper's business columnist and to his realtor. I had no problem 'bad-mouthing' Todd, using the facts, to anyone who'd listen, but certainly I hadn't talked to either his business columnist or his realtor."

Just three days after Vogt's combative call, Paul entered another boxing ring of sorts. On October 27, he attended his examination for discovery, an expensive fact-finding procedure that is a wide-ranging cross-examination just prior to a trial, with Hollinger's lawyer, Kevin Woodall.

Paul was exhausted after this day-long event in which he answered 537 questions posed by Woodall. "It was like a cat and mouse game," he says. "Their lawyer was questioning me in a very adversarial environment, trying to trap me or get me to agree to something that might weaken my case. It must be really tough and stressful for people who are trying to protect information or who need to lie to win."

That was not the case for us.

Standing up to Hollinger executives and their lawyers could be compared to challenging the schoolyard bully. Paul recognized their bullying tactics when he received a legal notice on November 2, 2000. It was a counter claim by LMPL/Hollinger, suing him for quitting. I just about went over the cliff when I heard this, but Paul remained calm and refused to be intimidated.

At the end of November, Paul left home for two weeks to check out the employment situation in Ontario. I did not cope well, despite having played the single-parent role many times before. My nerves were frayed. I was exhausted, fragile and vulnerable. I wrote about the experience in a column on November 26, with the headline, "Time Proved True Test of my Parenting Mettle":

I've just gone through what seemed like a two-week endurance test and, in many respects, I bombed. I was chief cook, bottle washer and chauffeur for the past 14 days while my husband was in Ontario. In my determination to keep the house in tip-top shape, the kids in line and my outside work accomplished, I overwhelmed myself. I realize now I had decided subconsciously to be super mom and in the process failed miserably to be the kind, nurturing mother I know I can be.

Those goofy things kids do like fight and argue; forget to bring their homework home and then forget to take it back to school; forget to go to the washroom before church and then make a scene because they can't hold it until the service is over; leave all the lights on while travelling from room to room; and slack off on their chores, became for me, while Paul was gone, criminal-code offences.

Stress reared its ugly head and had me in a stranglehold. As a result, I returned to my terrible, old habit of yelling at the kids. And they, in turn, yelled back. We had some good matches going and we all felt bad about it. We all missed Dad's calming influence and his refusal to get emotional when kids screw up. So without him, we all had a bit of an emotional meltdown.

I had an epiphany of sorts during those cold November days, one year after Paul's firing. I realized I was pretty good at rationalizing my behaviour. I realized I needed to take responsibility for my actions as a mother. I knew I had to stop blaming others for how I acted. I also came to realize a mother's true value lies not in how many tasks she can accomplish, but rather in how well she nurtures and fosters her children's self-worth. I also gained a true appreciation of families who endure regular, long separations due to their employment situations.

While he was in Ontario, Paul spent several days at Trajan Publishing, a publisher of hobby titles, of which we owned one-third. Paul Fiocca, business partner and Trajan operator, wanted Paul to do an evaluation of the business, including interviews with the 20 staff members. Fiocca, an extremely talented and bright individual, could perform most of the publishing functions himself. However, his weaknesses, some aspects of management and planning, were two of my husband's strengths. It was quite interesting to hear what the staff thought of the business and Fiocca's management of it. They felt controlled and underutilized. Fiocca was bewildered by this feedback. As a paternalistic manager who felt he carried the weight of the business on his back, he probably expected more praise for his efforts. He never said anything or commented on it, but this feedback might have influenced a decision Fiocca would make about four months later.

Bob Calvert, Radler's former deputy, responsible for many of Hollinger's Western Canada papers, called Paul at the beginning of November. When Hollinger sold those papers to CanWest earlier in the year, Calvert stayed on with CanWest in a senior role. He boosted Paul's sagging morale. He told Paul to "hang in." He gave Paul some hope that employment opportunities might open up for him. He said he would be glad to be a reference for Paul. He even said that he was in Radler's office when Radler saw Paul's letter claiming constructive dismissal.

"Calvert said he thought the letter was fine and that I just wanted to know what was going on," Paul remembers. Calvert seemed sympathetic to Paul's plight and genuinely interested in finding him a job.

At the end of 2000, The Daily Courier staff finally settled a new contract. Despite the fact that he had never been a fan of unions, Paul felt sorry for the Courier's unionized staff. They signed a five-year deal with no increases for the first four years and a mere two percent in the final year.

"The union and the Courier employees all figured Radler controlled both papers and that gave Radler *et al* an unfair advantage. Todd basically had a gun to the head of the union. I assume his approach was something like 'Accept this deal or I'll close the paper down,'" Paul hypothesizes.

Vogt had reported in one of his columns that the former owner, Thomson, had been ready to shut the paper down if Vogt hadn't come along and bought it. Whether that was true is anyone's guess, but fear was rampant among all newspaper employees in Kelowna at that time.

Rick O'Connor, Paul's boss from 1996 to 1998, had left LMPL just before Hollinger took control in early 1999. He took a job to head up David Black's Vancouver area newspapers. On December 12, O'Connor told Paul that he understood the Competition Bureau had ordered Radler to sell one of the two newspapers he was involved with in Kelowna. O'Connor added that both papers were listed with a well-known American-based newspaper merger and acquisition firm, Dirks, Van Essen &

Murray. This didn't come as a shock to Paul; it confirmed for him that the Bureau was forcing a sale.

Paul phoned the firm's president, Owen Van Essen, an acquaintance. "I asked him whether he had any papers for sale in Kelowna, and he said he might have. He said 'they' have labour and government problems but Van Essen thought he was being taken advantage of because he had been told to 'sit tight.' This seemed to confirm for me the Bureau told Radler to sell one of the papers, and I assumed Radler listed them with Owen to make things appear legitimate. But Owen wasn't allowed to actually sell them. More games."

As 2000 wound down and we welcomed in 2001, Vogt announced that he was expanding his operation, but there was no more talk of purchasing the Capital News or the Vernon Sun Review. Instead, he bought two small dailies in Medicine Hat and Lethbridge, Alberta, from Thomson.

We heard that financial information on the Capital News and the Sun Review had been passed along to a potential buyer and that a sale would be announced on January 5, 2001. Who could the purchaser be? It had been over a year since the Competition Bureau first started investigating the ownership question. Although Dirks, Van Essen & Murray had officially been given the job to sell one of the papers, Paul believed Vogt might be searching for possible buyers of the Capital News.

"This was no simple task," Paul says. "I'm sure they didn't want the paper in the hands of a company that could damage The Daily Courier any further. David Black of Black Press was the most likely buyer. He told me he had sent a letter of intent to Hollinger to purchase the Capital News, but had not heard back. Like Owen, David Black said he felt used."

Paul was still hopeful that he would hear something favourable on the job front from Calvert. He was disappointed when he received a call from the former Hollinger executive on January 15. Calvert explained that he couldn't do anything for Paul, because "you-know-who is still involved."

At that time, Radler and Conrad Black owned a chunk of CanWest and had a one-year management contract to operate the newspapers. Paul remembers, "A former colleague told me that Calvert took my situation all the way to the Asper family, who were the controlling shareholders of CanWest. Apparently their reply was they didn't want to rock the boat with Radler. It had been over a year since I had been fired and there weren't many viable employment opportunities for me."

Despite this bad news, Paul continued to hang on to the thought that they would be forced to sell to an established newspaper company, and he might be hired back. On the other hand, Paul intuitively felt Radler's ideal buyer would be someone who wasn't in the newspaper business...a buyer who didn't own a newspaper chain, but could be packaged to the Competition Bureau as an arm's-length owner.

Word leaked out that Bruce Hamilton, the high-profile owner of the Western Hockey League's Kelowna Rockets, was the prospective buyer. Who better than him, Paul thought. He was Vogt's friend. Vogt had written in his column about his friendship with Hamilton and had even taken steps within his newsroom to ensure the Rockets were given favourable coverage. Hamilton didn't even use the Capital News to promote his team, despite the fact the Capital News was the most dominant advertising medium in Kelowna. Hamilton had no newspaper industry experience that we knew of. He would probably need a lot of "advice."

Paul relays, "I called the Competition Bureau to fill them in on this information and I was told they would have a problem with a puppet owner, which it seemed Hamilton was about to become. I asked if they would provide me with a letter confirming the Bureau's involvement in the Kelowna newspaper business for use in my upcoming court case against Hollinger. My contact, Paul Feurer, told me because their work is done in confidence, he couldn't supply me with anything. He thought that if we got to trial, though, the Bureau might be forced to provide information. He finished by saying, 'Speaking personally, I admire what you've done ...you are very courageous.'"

In an earlier conversation, Feurer had told Paul that if Paul were ever to run for political office, he would be his campaign manager because everything Paul told him was factual. Aside from a handful of insiders who provided Paul with information, there were few cheerleaders along the way. Hearing this from someone in Feurer's position bolstered our spirits.

The Bureau called back and told Paul he had made some "interesting and valid" points regarding Hamilton. Paul was even more excited when our MP called him soon after. Werner Schmidt left a message saying Paul would be happy concerning the Competition Bureau's investigation of a local owner and that the Bureau would supply him with a letter concerning their involvement, something Paul could use at a trial. Schmidt had taken a genuine interest in what was going on and had leveraged some contacts within the top brass at the Bureau in Ottawa.

Days later, Paul heard from one of his former publishers that "the Hamilton deal is deader than a doornail." He was temporarily relieved, but quickly moved on to wondering, "Who now?" Surely Radler would try to find some other 'independent' to buy the paper at what would likely be a bargain-basement price.

A few days later, Paul did hear from the Bureau's Feurer and Andre Brantz. They told him they couldn't block a legitimate buyer from acquiring the Capital News. Paul asked them, "What if Hollinger financed the deal?" Brantz responded, "Do you think we'd allow that?"

Sources told Paul that Hamilton's deal had involved Hollinger financing and that may have been the reason for its collapse. Then another source warned Paul that they were trying to repackage the deal, explaining, "same animal but different clothes."

That news made us nervous, but we still held out hope the Hamilton acquisition would not happen.

XI

LEAVING PARADISE

"Coincidence is God's way of remaining anonymous."
- Albert Einstein

Our experience in Kelowna reminds me of the zip-lining adventure we had while vacationing in Costa Rica, long after we left B.C. The ride is exhilarating, but as the line comes to an end, the momentum wanes. You want to keep going, but you see the final platform and you know it's time to unhook and walk away.

Three significant events occurred on three consecutive days in March 2001, quite by coincidence. We could not ignore this accidental timing of circumstances; we took it as a sign it was time to take our leave.

My freelance writing assignments for the Capital News provided our only steady income in 2000, so it was a real concern when that weekly work seemed to be in jeopardy. Although my wage was not nearly enough to support our family (you don't get rich being a freelance journalist), I loved being a member of the media. Reporting suited my personality to a T. I loved meeting people, chasing a lead, finding a scoop, travelling, reading, writing, and broadcasting. Being a reporter satiated my curiosity and desire to seek the truth. On the lighter side, my anecdotal slice-of-life columns gave me an outlet to communicate with my readers in a humorous way.

I freelanced at the Capital News from the time Andrew Hanon hired me in 1998. I usually worked at home, a safe distance from office politics.

I had a great relationship with everyone and was assigned a wide variety of projects. The easy camaraderie I had with staff and managers might have lessened somewhat after Paul was let go, but my desire to contribute to the paper never wavered. Hanon had told me I would continue to work there as long as he was the editor, despite some very real pressure to get rid of me.

Hanon recalls that the very week after Paul was let go, Richard Sadick, then the acting publisher, approached him about me. "I remember he first asked me about whether the Family section was worth the expense," he recalls.

"I'm fuzzy on any exact words, but I do recall Richard suggesting that even if Family were to stay, perhaps Mary Lynn wasn't the person to be doing it. I vaguely recall him saying something about it being awkward having the ex-publisher's wife still wandering around the building. I knew that if I didn't nip this in the bud, I'd be answering leading questions every Monday from then on, so I dug in my heels and told Richard that Family was probably the most popular section of the paper, and Mary Lynn was doing a great job. She had a loyal following that we couldn't afford to lose. Period. Over the next several months, Richard would periodically suggest that Mary Lynn's column was no good and, not so subtly, ask me if I thought she should continue to be allowed to write it.

"That's about it. Mostly, I simply picked up on Richard's oh-so-delicate turns of phrase and body language that he didn't like having Mary Lynn roaming the halls like a spectral reminder of past evil deeds. And he certainly didn't want David Dodd ever to find out who she was."

By 2001, Hanon had left the paper to work in Alberta. The new editor, Barry Gerding, had difficulty understanding the complexities of Paul's case. I became leery when he hinted to me that he wanted to make changes to the Family section. He assured me I wouldn't be cut or cut back.

However, while chatting with me in his office on February 16, 2001, Gerding told me he could have scored big political points if he had gotten rid of me when he first arrived. He added, "But I like to think I'm above that." Although I sensed he was on my side, I was apprehensive about my future at the paper.

That was warranted. Shortly after that meeting, he told me that the Family section would be revamped to incorporate stories and columns on home renovation, decorating, and architecture, written by different freelancers. Then he dropped the bomb: I would contribute every other week. I informed him that I still wanted to contribute every week and that I was willing to revamp the section to be more lifestyles-oriented if that's what he wanted. I left his office under the impression that he was still open to me spearheading the content change and contributing copy every week.

I was hopeful that Gerding would not cave in to the pressure to get rid of me. After all, he himself had said that I was valuable and that there weren't many like me. I was shocked, then, when on March 9, I was told that, after 17 months, effective immediately, I would no longer be producing the Family section for the Capital News on a weekly basis. Gerding said he was still conflicted about how often he would run my column. He then asked if I wanted to write it for the following week. What I wanted to do was stay on, contribute every week, and make any changes they deemed necessary. I felt I was being forced out.

I left the building dazed, confused and angry. I didn't quite know what to do. With a lump in my throat, I went to do some school shopping for my kids. I didn't know what else to do after what seemed like a firing. Someone in senior management wanted me out because I was married to Paul, not because of any commitment or performance problems on my end. Within an hour, the conversation with Gerding had sunk in and I couldn't concentrate on anything else. I called Paul from a pay phone at the store. I started to cry as I relayed my plight. I kept looking over my shoulder to see if anyone was within earshot of my loud weeping.

"Mary Lynn, hang up and get home right now," Paul instructed me in a loving, but firm, tone.

To get a straight answer from Gerding, I wrote him to ask whether or not I could count on weekly work. I told him that I had worked an average of 30 hours a week for almost 18 months. I added that given my credentials, quality of work, and length of service, I needed to know why I was being cut back. He answered that I was still only a freelancer, though he wondered why I hadn't been a part-time employee. He explained that he could not guarantee me what I requested, but would like me in the trenches, "to fill in if needed" because, again, there weren't many "like" me.

To add insult to injury, I found out through the grapevine that there was a new freelancer and that she was a member of my book club. What an awkward situation! I felt like I was trapped in a bad soap opera.

The day after my breakdown on the phone with Paul, he received an email from Paul Fiocca, long-time operator of our hobby publishing company, Trajan, of which we still owned one-third. He told us that he was resigning. He wanted to maintain his ownership shares, but he no longer wanted to be the operator/publisher because he was burned out. He wanted to move to Windsor, where he would live with the woman he had been dating and now wanted to marry. We could not help but infer from his message that what he really wanted to say was, Hey, Paul, you're not working and you own part of this company. Why don't you move to St. Catharines and run it?

Paul had no interest in managing Trajan's five hobby magazines on coins, stamps, hockey cards, collectibles, and antiques. He knew he would never hire someone who, like himself, had no interest in, let alone a passion for, this type of publishing. This was a dilemma. Paul needed a job but the odds of finding a skilled publisher who had a genuine interest in these hobbies were low.

The next day, while Paul was contemplating how he could help solve the Trajan predicament, our real estate agent called. Bud Magrath said that the people who had expressed interest in buying our house several months earlier, when it was off the market, had tried to buy another one but that deal had fallen through. He asked if our circumstances had changed since we had rejected his clients' earlier inquiry. Well, yes, they had, Paul replied.

The week was a trifecta of developments. First, I lost my job and our only real source of income, then Fiocca resigned with no apparent replacement, and now we had an offer to buy our house, even though it wasn't on the market. Albert Einstein wrote, "Coincidence is God's way of remaining anonymous." These three seemingly unrelated events had us wondering: Was this God's way of saying, "Move on. You need to go back to Ontario?" We thought so. We agreed to sell the house and insisted on a June closing so our kids could finish their school year.

Spring was in full bloom. Paul decided to make one final attempt to draw Hollinger's CEO, Conrad Black, into the shameful activities happening in this tiny part of Black's massive media empire. Paul sat down to compose a letter to make him "officially" aware of what had taken place in Kelowna, even though Paul suspected Black had a good idea from the fax Paul had sent to Black's lieutenant, Don Babick, a year earlier.

On March 21, 2001, Paul wrote Black a four-page letter detailing what he knew about the dealings between Horizon and Hollinger. Paul wanted to ensure that Black would be on record as knowing what was taking place and Paul's assertion that Black or Radler or both had possibly breached their fiduciary responsibilities. Paul wanted to set the record straight, especially in light of the fact that at Hollinger's annual general meeting in the spring of 2000, Radler had described Paul as being a disgruntled employee who had resigned. Paul scrupulously outlined for Black the chain of events that had led to his claim of constructive dismissal.

Paul didn't expect Black to contact Radler, chastise him, and direct him to make amends. Paul didn't even expect to get a reply or an offer to settle. He simply wanted his side and assertions to be officially on the record. He sent the letter to Black's Canadian headquarters in Toronto via courier and confirmed it was signed for at Hollinger's end.

Neither Paul, nor his lawyer Alf Kempf, nor anyone else in the media knew at that time exactly how much of Horizon Radler and Black owned. Black had said at Hollinger's annual meeting in 2000 that he only owned a few shares. The true extent of their Horizon ownership would not be revealed until 2004, when Hollinger International's investigation by a special committee published a report indicating that Radler and Black were the significant owners of Horizon.

We didn't get a reply to Paul's letter, but two weeks after it was delivered, Kempf received news of an offer to settle. It was for $50,000, including all costs. We naturally wondered if Black had instructed Radler to get this settled, hoping to avoid any embarrassment or scrutiny over what was going on. The amount was insufficient, however, so we declined.

Then on April 3, 2001, an announcement was made that put a nail in the coffin of our unavoidable exit. Bruce Hamilton's West Partners consummated a deal to buy the Capital News and the Vernon Sun Review.

Paul was somewhat taken aback by the news, based on his communications with Werner Schmidt, who was then our MP, and with the Competition Bureau. That said, the Bureau did tell Paul it couldn't stop the sale to a legitimate buyer, whatever that meant. Ultimately, Hamilton's scant knowledge of the newspaper business, combined with his close ties to Horizon's president, Vogt, didn't disqualify him.

Hamilton, who was the company's president, told the Capital News staff that he had partners who preferred to remain anonymous. However, news editor Alistair Waters did a corporate search and found two other directors: Dave Dakers and Darryl Laurent.

Dakers was manager of the privately owned arena in Kelowna where Hamilton's hockey team played. Paul says, "When I first met Dakers, he made a number of disparaging remarks about the Capital News. I objected and we both ended up raising our voices, something I rarely do. My office manager, Karen Hill, heard the ruckus and came into my office following the meeting, wondering what had happened."

It was all so ironic. Hamilton and Dakers now owned the newspaper in which they had previously refused to advertise. It took a while before substantial information was unearthed about the third partner, Laurent who was the regional airport manager in Penticton B.C., about 60 km. south of Kelowna and, unbelievably, Todd Vogt's stepfather. Paul just about lost it when he heard this. How did this pass the Competition Bureau's criteria? What a cozy little club, Paul fumed: three owners who knew virtually nothing about the newspaper business, all connected to Vogt, the president of the competing paper.

"I was angry and frustrated," Paul admits. "With the help of many talented people, I'd spent my career building and fixing dozens of newspapers, all the while increasing shareholder value by tens of millions of dollars. After unsuccessfully trying to buy the papers I worked for in Ontario, I really thought I would have the opportunity to be an owner in the Kelowna operation. That was part of my reason for taking the Kelowna job. The folks who had hired me said ownership was a possibility. Now, after having worked so hard to make the Capital News highly profitable, West Partners, which had personal connections with Todd Vogt, was handed this sweetheart deal. And it only happened because I pestered the Competition Bureau to act to deny Radler's plans to consolidate the Kelowna newspaper market. Not only was I not an owner, I was out of job. Life isn't always fair; you have to play the cards you're dealt."

Paul had some interesting employment prospects in the United States, though. The first was a connection to the Seattle Weekly, owned by the Village Voice. Paul knew the company's president through Suburban Newspapers of America. Running an alternative weekly didn't seem like straight-laced Paul's type of product. That, combined with very expensive housing in Seattle, eliminated that possibility.

The other prospect came from a large, private-equity firm based in New York City. It had acquired a business called Lionheart Newspapers with three clusters of papers and printing plants in suburban Dallas/ Fort Worth, Minneapolis/St. Paul, and Kansas City. There were about 60 papers in total and the firm's partners were eager to talk with Paul.

They flew him in for an interview. He stayed in a hotel right across from the World Trade Centre, which four months later would fall to terrorists on 9/11.

Paul appreciates Americans' straightforward and no-nonsense way of conducting business, but didn't believe the position was right for him or for our family. He recalls, "They told me they wanted to make their money and get out in a couple of years. The message basically was they needed someone to increase profits quickly, which usually means cut staff. I'm not afraid to do that, if warranted, but I wasn't interested given that we were looking for a place to raise our children and somewhere where Mary Lynn and I could restart our careers."

Then there was the Trajan quandary. He hadn't committed to replacing managing partner Fiocca, but Paul had told his partners that he was committed to finding a solution.

Enter Mike Fredericks, a friend and colleague from Ontario, and owner of Annex Publishing, based in Simcoe, Ontario. Prior to our move to B.C., Paul had discussed becoming a partner with Fredericks. That hadn't gone anywhere, but this time, Fredericks was interested in buying Trajan and merging it with two other recently acquired businesses, specializing in automotive and aviation magazines. The plan was to merge all three businesses into one, perhaps based in Mississauga. Paul had a couple of major concerns about the Fredericks deal. One was his bonus plan; the other was the possibility of Trajan's staff having to relocate from their home base in St. Catharines.

When that deal fell apart, Paul accepted the publisher's role at Trajan. The collecting world, which includes everything from stamps and coins to Beanie Babies and hockey cards, was foreign to Paul. My perspective was that at least he would be making money for us, and not for a faceless, corporate entity. Throughout his career, he had made tens of millions for other owners; now, he would be working for a product in which he actually had some ownership. It was agreed that Paul would start work at Trajan on August 1, 2001. That would give us a little over a month to travel across the country in our tent trailer and to find a new house.

We said many emotional goodbyes to our neighbours, friends and work colleagues. On June 22, just one week before our departure, some of Paul's former staff members and managers organized a farewell party for us. It was both awkward and heartwarming. Some people we thought would want to say goodbye didn't show up, but we were surprised and pleased to see former Capital News publisher Jim Clark and editor Bryden Winsby, both of whom had left the paper soon after Paul's arrival. The guests presented us with two water-colour prints of the Okanagan, wonderful reminders of having lived in one of the most beautiful spots in Canada. Our favourite local artist, Alex Fong, presented us with one of his numbered prints, a fun and fanciful Okanagan Lake scene. We were truly honoured by this outpouring of affection. It reminded us yet again that it had never been our choice to leave.

With our house empty and every square inch vacuumed and wiped clean, I closed the front door behind me one last time. I tried to pull our family's imprints and energies from all the rooms, the yard, and the long, long driveway, and etch them into my mind's eye. I saw the kids playing ball hockey and building skateboard mazes, Andrew's pet rabbits running around the backyard after escaping from his homemade cages, the parties and games we had on the patio, and the neighbours' kids helping ours make an enormous teepee from fallen branches under a canopy of trees on our yard's hillside. When my brain was filled to the brim with visuals, I turned to Paul, who was standing silently beside me, and we reluctantly turned the key and locked the door.

The exploits and adventures we had on our 4,000-km road trip could fill another book entirely. It helped all of us recuperate spiritually and mentally, and gave us a wonderful break from stress and the Hollinger drama.

Paul received a couple of calls from our lawyer, Alf Kempf, during our travels. Kempf said he had completed a discovery of examination with Paul's former boss, David Dodd. Dodd had said he couldn't remember whether or not he consulted with Radler about Paul's letter claiming constructive dismissal/breach of contract and requesting a severance. But Paul knew better. He had a firsthand account from someone who had been in Radler's office when Dodd had come in to share and discuss Paul's letter.

During the other call, Kempf told us that Hollinger had verbally offered $100,000 "all in" to settle the matter. Maybe someone had decided it wasn't in their best interest to go ahead with this trial, after all. By now, though, Paul had mentally prepared himself and was eager to expose what Radler and Black were up to with Horizon. Again, he declined their offer.

XII

STRUGGLING TO FIND EQUILIBRIUM

"There are three constants in life ...
change, choice and principles." - Stephen Covey

The site we rented at Bissell's Hideaway near St. Catharines was tucked way back into the farthest corner of the trailer park. Although we had trees behind us for shade, we were situated in a spot that had no cross breeze. The summer of 2001 was a scorcher and our tent trailer, of course, had no air conditioning. I remember waking up many nights in a panic because in my semi-conscious state, I felt like I was in a sauna and starting to suffocate. Sweat would be pouring down my face and back. I'd throw back the top of my sleeping bag, thankful the rest of my family was slumbering soundly in the still and humid night.

Not only did I want a house with air conditioning, I wanted a job. I connected with Bob McKenzie, a publisher Paul had known while we were in B.C. We had learned that the gruff and burly newspaperman was now the publisher of the St. Catharines Standard. McKenzie laughed when I told him I wanted a job interview, if for no other reason than to get away from the kids and sit in an air-conditioned building. He hired me as a freelancer to do a weekly faces-and-places type of column, similar to what I had done in Kelowna. This was a perfect way to get to know local people. It permitted me to "party crash" various artistic events, festivals and fundraisers, take pictures of noteworthy people, and write up a story.

Bissell's Hideaway is part of the Town of Pelham, about 25 minutes from our Trajan business office in St. Catharines. Paul had his daily routine. After eating breakfast, he would gather up a handful of coins to operate the camp shower. He needed lots of change to keep it going long enough to get his shaving done. He'd curse if there weren't enough quarters in our little bowl because I had taken some to do the laundry.

Heading up our publishing business proved to be a shock to Paul's system. Small is not always easier or better. Over 12 years, our partner, Fiocca, had built up the company from two titles to five. A certified general accountant, Fiocca had been in the publishing business most of his life. He was smart and skilled at many of the technical aspects of publishing. He also had a genuine interest in collecting, especially coins and sports memorabilia.

Paul, on the other hand, doesn't have a "collector's gene" in his body. He could not muster any enthusiasm about these publications. Neither is Paul a "techie" – in fact, loading the photocopier was a mammoth challenge. He remembers his worst day of training. "I was learning how to mail catalogues we produced for a U.S.- based client. We crossed the border and drove over to an out-of-the-way Niagara Falls, N.Y., post office. There was no open space to spread out the envelopes containing the catalogues, so we stood in the blazing sun, at the back of Fiocca's sport utility, applying about eight stamps to each of the hundreds of envelopes. I wondered what on earth I had gotten myself into."

If the odd logistics weren't enough stress, Paul then discovered that Fiocca's positive outlook on Trajan's fortunes was not warranted. He remembers looking at the trend line on all five of the titles. Revenues for all of the magazines were in decline and expenses were climbing. The business had always been modestly profitable, but he saw that the margins had declined dramatically in recent years.

It was heading "south-east," a phrase used by Len Kubas, a friend and well known marketing and media consultant, to describe something going down. Fiocca didn't offer any explanation. He simply said to Paul, "This is small publishing. Get used to it."

100

A major shift was needed if the business were to survive. This was where Paul's expertise came to the fore. By looking at numbers, specifically market trends, Paul has an uncanny ability to predict how something will develop in the future. He's also good at assessing people and whether they're a good fit for the roles they're in. Fortunately, because he had done the consulting work for the business the year prior, he had a keen insight into our little business as well as its staffing situation.

Would the stormy seas in our life ever calm? Paul remembers the tempestuous period well. "I couldn't believe the mess I found myself in with our return to Ontario. We were living in a tent trailer with four kids between the ages of seven and fourteen. I was suing some of the most powerful people in the country and they were in turn suing me for quitting. Our savings had all but run out and the little business I thought was in really good shape was in fact bleeding cash."

The colour pink is said to have a soothing effect. One shade, known as "drunk-tank pink," is sometimes used in prisons to calm inmates. Arenas sometimes paint the visiting team's locker room pink to keep opposing players passive and less energetic. While pink's calming effect has been demonstrated, researchers of colour psychology have found that the effect occurs only during the initial exposure to it. When used in prisons, inmates often become even more agitated once they're accustomed to the colour.

At the eleventh hour, just before the kids had to start their new schools, on Labour Day, 2001, we moved into our new home. Yes, it was pink. Boy, was it pink. It boasted Pepto-Bismol-coloured walls, carpeting, kitchen countertops and ceramic flooring. It did, however, also boast the perfect size, layout, location, and living area for our needs. In very short order, the pink walls started to close in on us. Paul flew out to Vancouver the day after we moved in, because he had to participate in a second examination for discovery. During his two-day absence, the pink began to drive me insane. I wondered how Barbie had lived in that Dream House. The sooner we could find a painter, the better. Within the week, I had connected with one. She was booked solid, but took pity on me and made us her priority when she saw what we were living with.

Painting was underway on the morning of Tuesday, September 11, 2001, when the brutal murder of almost 3,000 innocent people through acts of terrorism on American soil shocked the world. Everything seemed to come to a standstill; everyone was numb with horror, then wracked with grief. When he was able to think clearly again, like many business owners, Paul wondered how that tragic day might negatively impact Trajan. 9/11 had changed everything, from our collective consciousness to commerce.

If our small, struggling hobby publications were to survive, Paul had to make some tough decisions. He decided to reduce staff by several members. In mid-October, following a shareholder meeting with his partners, Fiocca and Anderson Charters, five people were let go immediately. More dramatic organizational changes took place over the next two years. Bret Evans, the long-time editor of Canadian Coin News, described the company's structure up to that point this way: "We, the staff, were moons revolving around Paul Fiocca, the sun." No wonder Fiocca had burned out.

While trying to resume our business and personal lives, the day of reckoning finally came. In the dead of a bleak winter, with copious amounts of snow on the ground, Paul flew back to Kelowna to confront his adversaries.

XIII

PAUL THE PLAINTIFF

"When mores are sufficient, laws are not necessary;
when mores are insufficient, laws are unenforceable."

- Émile Durkheim

I had secretly prayed for two years that Hollinger and its executives would settle Paul's claim out of court and I was angry with God when Paul had to leave to go to court on January 21, 2002. Paul, on the other hand, anticipated this, expected it, and welcomed it. He was confident he would win and was excited at the prospect that all of the evidence of corruption would be on public record.

My trust in the Lord was evaporating and my hand had slipped from His. I was worried, anxious and fearful. I felt like Peter in the Bible's New Testament, who walked on water to meet Jesus, but started to sink when he lost faith. I was sinking, too. "Can we survive a loss?" I asked Paul.

"We have to survive; we have no choice. But we're not going to lose," Paul assured me.

With that, we resolved to fully embrace this journey, trusting God would reach out to catch us. We told ourselves that this challenge would make us stronger in character and in faith. Paul reminded me what doesn't kill you does make you stronger.

He admitted that he was perplexed about why Hollinger wanted to take him to court. They did make one last attempt, if you could call it that, on December 31, 2001, when they offered $1 to settle and avoid the trial that was just three weeks away. "We had turned down $50,000, and then $100,000 earlier in the year, so this was probably a last ditch attempt to see if I would bail with the trial getting so close," Paul muses.

Paul could only theorize. He surmised they knew he wouldn't sign a gag order limiting his ability to talk about what had occurred. After all, he had shown he was willing to walk away from not just his job in Kelowna, but a much bigger job as head of LMPL. He suspected that Radler wanted to make an example of him to other publishers who might not always unquestioningly go along with his wishes. Maybe Hollinger thought it could blow Paul away on the stand because it had the power and the money to hire big guns from a large Vancouver law firm.

Well, Goliath was in for a surprise: meeting David in the form of a small-town publisher and his small-town lawyer.

Paul flew to Kelowna on Saturday, January 19, and met with our lawyer, Alf Kempf, at Kempf's home, to go over final preparation for the trial on Monday. Paul wondered if he should claim punitive damages because of the circumstances. If they could prove that Hollinger had acted with malice simply because Paul told the truth, maybe he should receive more than the contractual one year of income they were fighting for. After all, Hollinger left our family high and dry. Kempf nixed this idea because he thought it would complicate and lengthen the trial and might hurt our chances of winning. He agreed that Hollinger's conduct was self-centred, but he was not certain it reached the bar of malice towards Paul.

Kempf wanted to keep the case airtight and keep Paul focused, because pursuing a constructive dismissal can be dangerous for an employee if he or she does not have all the facts. Common sense has to prevail. An employer is entitled to some leeway to conduct business and to make fundamental changes without giving rise to a claim for constructive dismissal, if the employer provides sufficient notice.

For a guy who had never been to court in his life, despite having to handle various libel suits served to him during his career as a newspaper publisher, this experience was scary, yet oddly exciting. Paul's adrenaline was flowing.

He stayed at a modest motel in a room with a small kitchen, and shopped across the street for his groceries. He continued to lean hard on his faith, keeping God at the centre of his world. On Sunday mornings, he ran about five kilometers through the snow to Trinity Baptist Church, where he sat at the very back of the balcony because he was in his running gear. Paul always enjoyed the messages given by Pastor Tim Schroeder, and the overall ambience and atmosphere of the big, "spirit-filled" church. He liked the physical building that resembled a theatre, rather than a traditional, icon-filled church. It had padded seats, stage lighting, and great acoustics for the singers and an orchestra of about 25 musicians.

The courtroom, on the other hand, was typical: a judge's bench, tables and chairs for lawyers sitting beside their clients, a witness stand, and benches for spectators, all beneath a high ceiling. Watching the proceedings were some reporters and, surprisingly, Todd Vogt, who had since moved away from Kelowna. At that time, he was flying in from California. Except for those couple of phone calls and sightings at Kelowna fundraising events, Paul had never had direct dealings with Vogt. He wondered why he was in the courtroom. He told me that maybe Vogt would testify and refute some of Paul's witnesses.

He was also surprised to see his former ad manager, Richard Sadick, sitting with Paul's former boss, David Dodd. At the time of the trial, Dodd was working in Chicago for Radler. Paul remembered that Sadick and Dodd were best friends when Dodd appointed Sadick publisher of the Capital News following Paul's departure. He also recalled that Sadick had revelled in his publisher role. Now, Sadick was the ex-publisher. He had been fired the previous October, just seven months after Bruce Hamilton of West Partners purchased the paper from Hollinger.

When Paul entered the courtroom on Monday morning, the Honourable Madam Justice Linda A. Loo, a B.C. Supreme Court judge from Vancouver, sat at her bench. This intense and solemn woman would preside over the civil case of plaintiff Paul Winkler v. defendant Lower Mainland Publishing Ltd., in the Supreme Court of British Columbia.

Paul immediately noticed how seriously she took her job. She made copious notes, stopping the proceedings to ask questions every time she did not fully grasp what was being said.

During the first three to four days of the trial, Paul provided his testimony and faced cross-examination by Hollinger's lead lawyer, Kevin Woodall. That proved to be a gruelling experience.

Kempf and his assistant, Rob Macleod, were extremely well prepared. During his testimony, Kempf asked Paul about everything from his employment history and the job he was hired to do, to the complexities of the marketplace and how a free-circulation community newspaper competed against a paid-circulation daily. Finally, Paul explained to the court how dramatically business had changed when Hollinger took over.

Kempf performed superbly, Paul told me, because he asked pertinent questions to elicit the whole story from Paul. This is vital, because as a witness, you are not allowed to have any documents on your lap to jog your memory. There was so much detail to provide for the record. Then, Kempf evoked some emotion from Paul when he asked about how rooted our four children had become in Kelowna. "My eyes watered spontaneously and I got choked up, excusing myself, feeling embarrassed. Later, I realized the incident let the judge know the toll this whole ordeal had had on my family," Paul observes.

Paul's diarized notes on what took place while he was working for Hollinger contained a lot of damning information. These notes had been considered evidence before the trial started and I had spent many painstaking hours transcribing them and typing them. However, during Paul's second day on the stand, Woodall asked to have them removed from the evidence file. Hollinger's lead lawyer claimed they weren't contemporaneous because some of Paul's notations were added in a margin after the date of the event. Woodall also took issue with the fact that they were written in pencil, which can of course be erased, and he suggested they were self-serving. Had Paul known when he was writing them that they would become evidence in a court case, he would have used a pen and he would not have added notes in the margin.

Justice Loo didn't seem to be buying Woodall's argument of inadmissibility, but said she'd make a ruling about them later.

Woodall's cross-examination of Paul continued after lunch on the second day and well into the third. Having been through two discoveries, Paul was well acquainted with Woodall's adversarial approach. He was relentless, but he couldn't poke holes in any of Paul's testimony. At one point, he accused Paul of planting with SILK-FM the startling story that he had been fired. Woodall said Paul was a good friend of the reporter at the radio station. That was false. Paul was sure it was Vogt who leaked the story, either directly or indirectly. He looked at him from the witness stand and said defiantly, "Nice try, Todd."

Woodall then seemed to change his approach. He brought up the fact Paul had sometimes referred to Vogt as "Pinocchio" around the Capital News office. Paul didn't deny it because Capital News editor Andrew Hanon came up with the nickname. Woodall suggested it was unprofessional behaviour for someone in a publisher's position. He continued in this vein, accusing Paul of also acting unprofessionally when he discussed his concerns about Horizon and Vogt with his first boss, Rick O'Connor, who had moved over to work with Black Press. He said Paul should not have revealed his concerns to a competitor.

At this point, the judge intervened to remind Woodall that this was a trial to determine whether Paul had resigned or had been constructively dismissed; it was not about whether he had been let go for cause. Woodall assured her that was not his motive, but continued to press on in this vein. Kempf objected and the judge wasn't buying Woodall's new tactic, so she called a lunch break and suggested the lawyers sort this out. She told Woodall she hadn't seen anything in the plaintiff's conduct to suggest Hollinger had a case to claim cause.

Woodall returned from the break saying he was not alleging cause, but rather repudiation of contract. This seemed like a reversal from his earlier position, but at least it was clearly confirmed that cause was not being argued. Paul's time on the stand was almost over. The first of his witnesses needed to be squeezed in on day three.

Paul was and remains very grateful to the men who were brave enough to appear as his witnesses. Some were still directly connected to Hollinger, but even those who weren't could easily have found themselves in association at some point because the industry was small and consolidation was ramping up.

His first witness was Rick O'Connor, Paul's direct boss when he was first hired by LMPL. Just months before Hollinger took control of LMPL, O'Connor left to work for David Black. O'Connor's testimony centred mainly on why LMPL decided it needed a general manager for its growing business in the B.C. interior and why Paul was selected for that role. He also talked about the circumstances surrounding Paul's acceptance of the temporary role of publisher of the Capital News.

O'Connor said the company hired Paul because of his experience, passion, and competitive, take-no-prisoners approach. He also said Paul worked extremely hard and surpassed company expectations. He said they only disagreed on the amount of reporting to him that Paul should do. He understood Paul was extremely independent and not used to reporting to a boss very often. O'Connor said that was resolved and they had a good relationship.

Paul called me every night to give an update on the proceedings. That helped me enormously. Not being with my husband during this crucial time upset me. I could not concentrate on anything and had to walk the block around our house almost every hour. I seemed to be endlessly blinking back tears. After his time on the stand on day four, Paul told me he was exhausted but assured me that all was well. His story was now on record. Hollinger's lawyers had not been able to discredit anything he had said, despite coming at him from every possible angle. Paul was satisfied. Kempf, on the other hand, would occasionally get a bit frustrated with Paul, who was trying to get on record everything Hollinger was up to, including how the Capital News had found its way into Bruce Hamilton's hands. Kempf wanted to stay focused on the constructive dismissal claim. He reminded Paul that the goal was to win this case, not to be a crusader. That turned out to be sage advice.

Chartered accountant Orest Smysnuik was unequivocally Paul's most valuable witness. The chief financial officer for LMPL provided what Paul thinks might have been the most useful and helpful piece of evidence in the whole case. Smysnuik confirmed that he was with Paul when Dodd told him to "think outside the box," and to "look into setting up a press in a barn," presumably to print competitor Vogt's privately owned Daily Courier.

When Smysnuik appeared at the trial, he was no longer directly under Hollinger's control because his operation had been sold to CanWest. However, he took a considerable career risk by showing up. He testified that Dodd had told him Vogt was on a leash, and that he had assumed Dodd had meant Radler had Vogt on that leash. He confirmed that he and Dodd had discussed appointing Paul president of LMPL's newspapers.

Following his final meeting with Dodd in Vancouver, Paul had gone out to dinner with Smysnuik. Smysnuik testified that at that dinner, Paul clearly sensed his time with LMPL was coming to an end. Smysnuik also testified that Vogt had called him early in 2000, just after Paul's firing, requesting financial information on the Capital News. That was around the same time that Vogt was spreading rumours about purchasing the Capital News.

Next up was Andrew Hanon, who flew in from Edmonton. Paul considered Hanon a principled man and an honourable journalist. He had appointed him Capital News editor soon after Paul took over as temporary publisher. Hanon left the paper in late 2000 to work for Duff Jamison in suburban Edmonton. Hollinger owned a big chunk of Jamison's Great West Publishing operation, which made testifying awkward for Hanon. In fact, about one week before testifying, he got a call from Dodd, who asked what he would be testifying about. Hanon thought that had been an attempt to intimidate him.

Hanon and Paul had shared the same vision for the Capital News and the basic philosophical tenets of journalism: honesty and objectivity. When Kempf asked Hanon about the changes Paul had made at the paper, Hanon replied, "Well, it was, it was miraculous, really. He energized the staff. He gave everyone a sense of purpose. He turned things around financially. In the newsroom itself, we were actually inspired enough to do more with less."

Hanon recalled what happened when Hollinger took control of the paper late 1998. He even remembered Radler's visit to the Capital News just before they took ownership, when Radler told the management team that the Capital News wasn't a real newspaper.

He verified the story about Vogt trying to cancel Roger Ebert's column in the Capital News and switch it to Vogt's Daily Courier. Hanon said to the court that Vogt had told the company who distributed the column that there was a common owner of the Courier and the Capital News and that's why the column could now appear on The Daily Courier's pages instead.

During one of his calls home, Paul relayed that the defence lawyers seemed to be baffled and surprised by the testimony of his next witness, Russ Niles. Niles had worked for Paul at the Vernon Sun Review, only to be lured away and hired by Vogt in 1999, to be managing editor of Vogt's newly established Vernon Times. Niles lost his job around the time the daily folded, six months later. Niles, an excellent investigative reporter, had become aware of Vogt's duplicity and was eager to expose him.

Niles testified that Vogt told him that Radler had instructed Vogt to buy the Kelowna Capital News and the Vernon Sun Review. This happened during Radler's visit to Kelowna in November 1999 and the same day that Radler came to the Capital News to tell Paul that Todd was "a good boy" and not to be "so hard on him." Hearing this made sense to Paul; it was soon after Radler's visit that Vogt started telling anyone who would listen that he was buying his competitors in Kelowna and Vernon.

Niles also testified that he heard Vogt leave a message for Brian Brownfield, at that time a salesman for the Vernon Sun Review. Brownfield had apparently turned down Vogt's job offer to work at his new daily. Miffed, Vogt left a threatening voice message implying that Brownfield would soon find himself out of a job. Gary Johnston, who was then the publisher of the Sun Review, had told Paul about this when it happened. Niles, however, had actually heard Vogt leave the message.

Then the kicker: Niles said he had knowledge of Paul's departure from the Capital News before Paul knew. Niles said he had been in Vogt's Daily Courier office late in the afternoon of November 17, the same day Paul faxed his letter claiming constructive dismissal to Dodd. Niles said Vogt told him that the bankers had approved his acquisition of the Capital News and the Sun Review, and that all that was now required was Hollinger board approval on December 5. Vogt also flippantly crowed to Niles that Paul Winkler was "history" or "outta there."

A few minutes later, Niles chatted with other newsroom employees at The Daily Courier, and they all seemed to know what Niles had just learned. Niles was also present at a B.C. Labour Board hearing in Vancouver later in 2000 where Vogt testified that he had indeed made an offer to buy both papers, but the Hollinger board had turned it down on January 25, 2000.

Before Woodall cross-examined Niles, he wanted a break. Paul thought it odd, but guessed that Woodall had not been prepared for this evidence. Vogt probably had not informed him about his newsroom chat with Niles. Paul assumed that Radler did not know either, and would not be pleased about it.

Paul told me that Vogt had been in and out of the courtroom throughout the trial up to this point. He said that Vogt always had a cell phone in hand and he and Kempf believed Vogt was calling Radler to give him updates. Vogt was expected to testify and Paul was eager to see him on the stand. I did not share Paul's enthusiasm; this news alarmed me because neither did I trust Vogt nor consider him genuine. When court resumed, Paul said Hollinger lawyer Woodall came out with guns blazing. Forceful and aggressive, he started by noting that Niles was suing Vogt and Horizon for wrongful dismissal, slander and defamation. Woodall suggested Niles had an axe to grind with his former employer and alleged that he was lying.

Woodall described Niles as "a junior manager." Niles, he said, would be someone with whom Vogt would have had little contact, and someone in whom Vogt would not confide. Woodall stated that Niles' testimony on this was a willful and deliberate fabrication. To this, Niles replied, "You're calling me a liar?"

"Yes, I am," Woodall responded.

Niles protested but kept his cool.

Woodall kept on this line of questioning, suggesting that someone like Niles would not be privy to Vogt's acquisition and financing plans. Again, Woodall said Niles' testimony was a willful and deliberate fabrication. This time, Niles blew up. Raising his voice, he said, "There you go calling me a liar again. I'm not a liar, sir."

"Yes, I am calling you a liar."

Niles again emphatically stated that he was not lying. Finally, the judge stepped in. Paul knew the testimony Niles supplied had been damaging to Vogt.

Paul's fifth and final witness was Alan Monk, the manager of the Capital News' highly successful, weekly real estate publication. Vogt had attempted to hire him. Again, in Monk's testimony, the fuzzy ownership lines between Horizon and Hollinger were reported to the court. Monk said Vogt assured him during their first meeting that Horizon and Hollinger were completely separate. However, at a later meeting, when Monk said he expressed concern to Vogt about the viability of his operation, Vogt asked him, "How long do you think it will be before I play the Radler card?"

Monk also testified that in July 2000, then-publisher of the Capital News, Richard Sadick, had said something disturbing to him. Sadick had heard that Paul had approached some of the managers to provide him with letters about what had happened while he was in charge. He had also asked them to possibly testify in court as witnesses for him. Sadick said to Monk, "I'll go straight to David Dodd and, well, those guys are ruthless, they'll find a way to get you out of here in a real hurry."

Those words must have echoed in Monk's mind the week before his testimony. Like Hanon, Monk had received a phone call from Dodd inquiring about what he would be saying in court. Monk said the call was very unnerving, because he knew his job and career were likely still under Radler's influence.

With Paul's testimony and his witnesses' accounts in the can, he couldn't wait to hear what his former employers had up their sleeves; especially David Radler. During the first day of the trial, Paul learned that Radler, Todd Vogt, and Richard Sadick were expected to testify. Paul was surprised that Radler, well-known for avoiding public appearances, wanted to testify for the defence.

Why would Radler, Conrad Black's long-time partner, deputy chairman, president and chief operating officer (COO) of a $2-billion corporation, waste his time with a lowly, weekly newspaper publisher's wrongful dismissal case over a mere one year of income? Did Paul's allegations concern him that much? Paul speculated that Radler wanted to refute anything Paul had said that might damage Hollinger or him.

The defence case kicked off quietly and uneventfully when Hollinger's first witness, Alison Yesilcimen, was called to the stand. She had been hired to replace Vogt as publisher of The Daily Courier when he went to California. Yesilcimen had worked for ADitus, Hollinger's corporate sales division, located in Vancouver in the same small building where Radler and Dodd had their offices. That was the reason she was testifying.

Paul alleged that Hollinger-owned ADitus demonstrated impropriety when it showed favouritism to Vogt's paper over his, the Hollinger-owned paper, when pitching major advertising accounts. Yesilcimen testified that when she worked for ADitus, there was no such wrongdoing. Paul didn't have a witness to back up his claim, and while he believed it to be true, it's one argument that probably ended in a draw.

On day five of the trial, Friday, January 25, there was a buzz in the courtroom. More spectators had shown up, including many reporters and a camera crew waiting outside the courthouse. It was Radler's turn on the stand, having just arrived in town on his roomy, private jet.

On the stand, Radler explained that Hollinger owned between 500 and 600 newspapers around the world. Woodall quickly, and somewhat surprisingly, asked the question we all wanted an answer to: How much of Horizon did he and Conrad Black own? No doubt Woodall wanted to get it out of the way, knowing they'd be forced to divulge it under cross-examination. Radler replied 48 per cent, with each owning 24 per cent. He continued on to say that he thought Vogt had 35 per cent, and that other individuals associated with Hollinger owned the remaining shares.

Incredibly, this was the first time anyone had heard the amount of their holdings. Paul was shocked. Vogt had always given the impression he was the controlling, if not sole, shareholder of Horizon and that Radler and Black had nothing to do with Horizon. Paul couldn't believe what he was hearing. He had thought Vogt did have control of Horizon, but that Radler and Black had some kind of deal that allowed them to tell Vogt what to do.

And, of course, Paul remembered that Conrad Black, when questioned about his possible ownership of Horizon at the May 2000 Hollinger annual meeting said he had a few shares. "When I learned," Paul said, "that Radler and Black essentially controlled Horizon, because all they needed was the vote of one of their other minority shareholders to outvote Vogt, I thought, surely this was an issue for security regulators.

"Radler and Black privately owned a paper that was in direct competition with one owned by Hollinger, the public company they had a fiduciary responsibility to operate for the good of those shareholders."

Woodall led Radler through a series of questions, allowing Radler to provide reasons for his actions. He said that neither he nor Conrad Black were involved in the operation of Horizon, and that he was surprised to hear Vogt had launched the new daily newspaper in Vernon without telling him. Paul almost burst out laughing. On other matters, such as Competition Bureau rules and regulations, Radler said he had no concerns about running afoul of them. On the matter of getting his publicly traded newspaper, the Capital News, to print its competitor, The Daily Courier, in the event of a strike, Radler said that was Hollinger's policy.

He also said he had little knowledge of Paul's issues as they related to Horizon. He said he recalled Dodd telling him about Paul's letter claiming constructive dismissal, but that he was not involved in the decision to "accept Paul's resignation." On the stand, under Woodall's questioning, he basically denied any wrongdoing or involvement.

When Woodall asked Radler why he had played down his and Black's ownership in Horizon, Radler said he hadn't, it simply hadn't been an issue. Radler also claimed he knew nothing about Vogt's offer to buy the Capital News in late 1999. He did admit that Hollinger had loaned Horizon $8 million and that Vogt had been calling him throughout the first four days of the trial giving him updates, but Radler denied that he was instructing the lawyers.

We didn't know too many Kelowna natives; many of the residents there come from somewhere else. But Kempf was born and raised in Kelowna. He was a farm boy who grew up on an orchard. When we first met him, he did not display what one typically thinks of as being a lawyer's personality. He wasn't outgoing, aggressive or argumentative.

Kempf had accepted Paul's suggestion of contingency fees, which meant our legal fees would be contingent upon some recovery or award in Paul's case. No doubt he would have preferred to charge his regular hourly rate. They had struck an agreement whereby Kempf would charge a reduced hourly rate and receive a percentage of any award Paul might receive from the court. We believe he was vested in Paul's case, despite knowing how difficult it would be to go up against one of the biggest media empires in the world and its team of lawyers. Kempf had prepared well. Very well. What Paul did not expect was Kempf's brilliant performance.

But he was brilliant, especially cross-examining Hollinger's witnesses. Under Kempf's cross-examination, Radler said he thought that the Competition Bureau would allow a common owner of both papers in Kelowna. Then, in a dazzling move, Kempf followed that up by asking, "If that were the case, why didn't Hollinger buy The Daily Courier from Thomson instead of Horizon?" If Radler had been looking out for

Hollinger and its shareholders, he would have pursued that approach, would he not? Radler said Hollinger wasn't buying small newspapers at that time.

Kempf wanted to know what communication Hollinger had with the Competition Bureau following Paul's dismissal. Woodall strongly objected, saying that such communication took place after Paul was gone and was not relevant to his case. The judge considered this and, to Paul's delight, allowed Kempf to pursue the line of questioning. Radler remained vague about exactly what took place, but admitted that the Competition Bureau had been asking questions and that, as a result, Hollinger decided to sell the Capital News. Radler said they did so because they didn't want to upset the government agency, particularly when Hollinger was in the process of selling almost all of its Canadian newspaper holdings to CanWest for $3.3 billion. They needed Competition Bureau approval.

While listening to Radler's testimony, Paul gained a clearer picture of what he thought Radler had intended to do: to sell the Hollinger-owned Capital News to his privately owned Horizon Daily Courier, then pocket the substantial gains personally, the considerable gains that can be reaped without direct competition.

Paul's view was that Radler hoped that the deal was small enough that the Competition Bureau wouldn't get involved or, as Dodd had put it to Paul, that it was probably "beneath their radar." To pull this off, Radler also had to ensure the Capital News was available for Horizon to buy. That was somewhat difficult because Hollinger was doing deals that involved the Capital News' parent company, LMPL. Radler twice had the Capital News excluded from deals that involved the other LMPL papers.

Meanwhile, Kempf tried to pin Radler down on why the Capital News had been left out of the Income Trust that Hollinger had put together in 1999, when it included all of the other B.C. papers owned by LMPL. Radler claimed the earnings weren't high enough to justify the price they were getting. To Paul, that simply didn't make sense; many of the other papers in the package had much lower earnings.

Then Kempf asked Radler why, at a later date, the Capital News was one of a handful of papers not purchased by CanWest. Radler claimed that CanWest didn't want the paper. Again Paul was puzzled; why wouldn't CanWest want the paper when it owned the local TV station, CHBC?

At the lunch break during the proceedings, Paul watched in disbelief as Radler, who had just been grilled by Kempf during cross-examination, asked our lawyer out for lunch. Kempf refused. Paul was aghast at Radler's chutzpah.

Kempf finished up his cross-examination by asking Radler to comment on whether several quotes attributed to him were true. One quote was from Conrad Black, who said, "Radler used to regularly quote from a 19th century manual on industrial relations that began with the premise that all employees are slothful, incompetent and dishonest."

The other quote was found in an early 1992 Maclean's magazine article, outlining Radler's explanation of the company's editorial policy: "If editors disagree with us, they should disagree with us when they're no longer in our employ." Paul couldn't help but think that was precisely what had happened to him.

Radler did not answer the question directly. Instead, he kept asking to see the articles and to give the context in which they were written.

Court was adjourned until Monday morning.

Paul spent much of that weekend considering what Vogt and Sadick might say in Hollinger's defence and what material he could provide Kempf to counter it. On the phone with me, Paul's voice sounded more confident and electrified. After each and every conversation, the yoke around my neck felt lighter and lighter. He wished I were there with him and provided me the colour commentary to help me visualize the scene.

To his shock, neither Vogt nor Sadick appeared on Monday, even though both had been there the previous week. Neither would be testifying. On one hand, Paul was relieved but, on the other, he had been looking forward to Kempf's cross-examination of them.

Finally, David Dodd, Paul's former boss, took the stand. A chartered accountant, Dodd was the key witness to defend Hollinger's actions. Woodall walked Dodd through his recollection of the events that led up to Paul's departure. For the most part, Dodd denied most of the incriminating statements he had made or he said that he didn't remember.

Paul chuckled when Dodd tried to explain away one of the key pieces of evidence that had been corroborated by Paul's witness, Smysniuk, the week before. It was the infamous request from Dodd that Paul set up a "press in a barn" to print Vogt's paper.

Dodd's explanation was pretty lame but, under the circumstances, it was probably the best he could come up with. He told the court that Hollinger owned a regional printing plant in West Frankenfurt, Illinois in a large, rectangular building. When Woodall asked if it had a nickname, Paul knew where this was going and almost guffawed. Dodd replied that yes, indeed, it was called "the barn."

He went on to explain that that was what he meant when he suggested that Paul set up a press in a barn; that Paul should look into printing some of Hollinger's Lower Mainland sister papers in a new, larger printing facility because some of them had been farmed out to other printers.

This notion wasn't just amusing; it was completely implausible. Why would the Capital News print newspapers in Kelowna and truck them back to Vancouver, four hours away, on a mountain highway that was often closed due to extreme weather? Paul didn't think the judge bought Dodd's story, either.

The comic relief got even better during Kempf's cross-examination. One conversation went like this:

Kempf: "Mr. Winkler said in his direct evidence that you referred to Mr. Todd Vogt as a 'kiss-ass,' do you recall that?"
Dodd: "I do recall the evidence."
Kempf: "Yes, and you did do that. You referred to Mr. Vogt as a 'kiss-ass,' correct?"

Dodd: "I – I – I'm not sure – I heard the evidence. I was not clear under what circumstances Mr. Winkler maintains that I said that."

Kempf: "Well, just answer the question. Did you ever tell Mr. Winkler that you referred to Mr. Vogt as a 'kiss-ass' or thought him to be a 'kiss-ass'?"

Then Kempf asked him what a "kiss-ass" means. Dodd squirmed in his seat and repeatedly asked Kempf if he could re-phrase the question or let him write down the question. The "kiss-ass" exchange covered five pages of court documents. Dodd would not give a straight answer and did not admit on the stand that he ever made such a statement to Paul. He did say that people may regard Todd as a "kiss-ass" and may regard him as a "kiss-ass," too.

For Paul, this exchange provided temporary levity.

During a break, Kempf leaned over to Paul and asked in disbelief, "Why are they doing this?" meaning, why did they take this to court? Paul shook his head. He couldn't believe it, either. They didn't seem to have any good explanation for their actions and at times they looked downright goofy.

Kempf wrapped up his cross-examination and the trial itself by noting that he had started with questions concerning "kiss-asses." He finished by asking Dodd if anyone ever called Mr. Winkler a "kiss-ass." Dodd said he didn't know. Kempf then suggested that Hollinger fired Paul because he wasn't a "kiss-ass" and had refused to cooperate with Vogt and their plans for Kelowna. Dodd denied it, but it was a powerful conclusion.

After the trial, Paul told me he was pleased that Dodd acknowledged that Paul was on track, just prior to his departure, to become the president of LMPL, the Capital News' parent company of about 1,000 employees. He was amazed, however, when Dodd testified that he didn't know about Radler's ownership in Horizon.

We were also still stunned about Radler's admission that he and Conrad Black owned 48 per cent of Horizon. We assumed when Black said back at the Hollinger annual meeting in May 2000 he had "a few" shares that meant maybe three or four per cent. Twenty-four per cent is more than "a few" by most standards and we wondered what else these guys would lie about.

We would find out in 2004 that Radler and Conrad actually owned 73 per cent of Horizon and that, shockingly, David Dodd, too, owned some shares. Too bad we hadn't thought to ask him if he owned any shares at Paul's trial.

The trial was over but Kempf, who had turned out to be far from a local yokel, still had his work cut out for him. Both sides had agreed to document their closing arguments for the judge within the next two weeks. They had also agreed to limit this to a maximum of 30 pages. When Woodall submitted his, it was 58 pages, almost double what they had agreed on. Such arrogance!

Our future was now in the hands of one person: Madam Justice L.A. Loo of Vancouver.

XIV

A PYRRHIC VICTORY

"The right thing to do and the hard thing to do
are usually the same."

- Steve Maraboli, Life, the Truth, and Being Free

It was the dog days of mid-summer 2002 and still no judgment. We had expected a decision by June at the latest. Months had passed since the trial. We were troubled and wondered if this length of time was a good or bad sign. Our financial situation was grim. Thankfully, my dad had given us a loan. Even if we did win our case, though, would Hollinger appeal on some technicality and continue the bullying? Many industry insiders told Paul that Hollinger would surely appeal. Could we survive financially and emotionally?

By July, we surmised we would not hear from Justice Loo until September. We were surprised, then, when we received an email message from our lawyer in the middle of August. Paul was alone the day it arrived. At first, he thought it was bad news, because there was no mention of a victory. It simply said the judge had rendered her decision and directed him to click on an electronic link to read the judgment.

Paul followed the link and, with some trepidation, began reading. Nothing about winning ...nothing about winning ... It was only when he scrolled to the end that he discovered he had been successful. He cheered as loudly as he could and made himself a "man-sized Manhattan cocktail" to celebrate.

In the 35-page decision, the judge highlighted the key points of her findings. She ruled that Paul had in fact been told to set up a press in a barn to aid Horizon in the event of a labour disruption. This was critical evidence because it clearly showed that Paul had been asked to aid a competitor. Had Orest Symsniuk, LMPL's VP of finance, not corroborated this, we doubt the judge would have been able to agree with Paul's testimony on this key point.

She then described LMPL president David Dodd's testimony:

On cross-examination, Mr. Dodd was extremely uncomfortable and skirted around questions he did not want to answer. Often, he insisted on writing down, word for word, fairly simple questions, before he would answer, and when he finally answered, his answer was not responsive. At times I had the distinct impression he was reconstructing the evidence, or reluctant to answer the question because the answer would not be favourable for him or LMPL.

She complimented Paul:

I find that Mr. Winkler had a much better recollection of the events and the sequence of events than did Mr. Dodd. That may be a result of Mr. Dodd having to attend to all of LMPL's operations, not just the Okanagan, and the fact that Mr. Winkler made notes of the events as they occurred. However, I have no hesitation in finding that where there is a conflict between the evidence of Mr. Winkler and Mr. Dodd, I prefer and accept the evidence of Mr. Winkler.

She said that Paul had excellent leadership skills, and that he had worked hard and aggressively. She rendered her decision stating:

I am satisfied that the plaintiff has established all the material facts alleged to amount to a constructive dismissal. I accept Mr. Winkler's evidence that he had no intention of resigning. Rather, he thought from his November 4, 1999 meeting that his employment relationship with LMPL was close to an end. As he put it, he thought they wanted him out of the marketplace. His main concern was ensuring that LMPL lived up to its contractual severance obligation and he wanted to move the 'process' along.

I find that Mr. Dodd knew that Mr. Winkler did not intend to resign, and that the letter of November 17, 1999, did not amount to a resignation. Rather, at the meeting of November 4, 1999, Mr. Dodd was, to use his words, 'shocked' and his 'antennae started to quiver' on hearing that Mr. Winkler had an employment contract and had sought legal advice. I find that Mr. Dodd decided then and there to put the promotion permanently 'on hold,' because he knew nothing about the contract and he thought Mr. Winkler 'was trying to set up a financial claim.'

I find it surprising that Mr. Dodd claims he interpreted Mr. Winkler seeking legal advice as meaning that there was some issue that Mr. Winkler chose not to speak to him about, when almost in the same breath he admits that Mr. Winkler should ask few questions and stick to his knitting.

Mr. Winkler did nothing wrong by seeking legal advice. However, Mr. Dodd thought it was wrong, and that it had irretrievably harmed the employment relationship. Instead of terminating Mr. Winkler's employment and providing 12 months' salary, Mr. Dodd took the opportunity of using Mr. Winkler's letter of November 17 -- which Mr. Dodd described as 'a lawyer's letter' -- as his resignation. In his notes in preparation for a meeting with the staff at the Daily (sic, this should read Capital News), Mr. Dodd wrote, 'Today I have accepted Paul's resignation. It will probably be a dogfight.' It would be a dogfight because Mr. Dodd knew that Mr. Winkler did not resign.

As far as the credibility of the witnesses was concerned, Justice Loo said:

Mr. Winkler is, as Mr. O'Connor testified, extremely passionate about his work and extremely competitive. He saw the Daily as the Capital's main competitor. I find Mr. Winkler highly ethical, and acutely aware of what he thought he could do, or not do, within the confines of the law. He asked many questions and received few satisfactory answers; at least, none from Mr. Dodd.

Mr. Dodd's communication style is radically different from Mr. Winkler's. Mr. Dodd said that Mr. Winkler was quite emotional about his job. Mr. Dodd describes himself as 'unemotional about business matters.' It is an apt description. At times in giving evidence, he was brusque and overbearing. To his credit, Mr. Dodd is an extremely capable lieutenant who asks few questions, and carries out the orders of his superior.

At trial, Mr. Dodd denies telling Mr. Winkler ownership of the Daily was beneath the radar of the Competition Bureau, while on examination for discovery he admits that he possibly made the comment. He also admits that he told Mr. Winkler when he was asking questions about ownership and control of the Daily that he should 'stick to his knitting.' He denies telling Mr. Winkler that he was working in an 'artificial environment' although I find that he did.

At trial, counsel for LMPL objected to the admissibility of Mr. Winkler's contemporaneous notes. In view of my findings on credibility, I do not find it necessary to determine the admissibility of the notes.

Paul was awarded $160,495.64, most of which was his salary and bonus for one year as had been stated in his contract. He was also awarded costs and interest. But would Hollinger appeal the judgment as most insiders had predicted? It had several months to do that, so we remained on pins and needles wondering what the next chapter in this never-ending ordeal would be.

In the days following the B.C. Supreme Court judgment of Winkler v. Lower Mainland Publishing Ltd., several newspapers reported on it. The Globe and Mail and Vancouver Sun each interviewed Paul and published stories. They could best be described as David (Paul) versus Goliath (Hollinger) reports. The Record, the daily in our former hometown, also published Paul's victory, but not one print or broadcast outlet investigated further. Paul pleaded with reporters to dig further into the story and to research the links between Horizon and Hollinger, and Radler and Black's ownership and connections. Surely, he thought, if the media thought he was fighting some mythical dragons before his trial, his triumph in court would prove that he was on to something.

We were disappointed and disillusioned. The media are quick to report on misdeeds in institutions such as banking, politics, and other large corporations, but apparently not eager to make similar revelations about their own industry.

Paul was disheartened and perplexed by the lack of interest in what had been exposed at his trial. On the surface, it may have looked like a simple, wrongful dismissal case, but on any further examination, it was clearly significantly more. He felt his case had more than enough evidence to warrant further investigation into whether the top two executives in Canada's largest media company may have committed securities fraud. Was it just too unfathomable for big-city media types to imagine that Radler and Black were possibly committing an offence in relatively small and remote Kelowna, B.C.? Or they were afraid to probe further, given the duo's propensity for civil action lawsuits and their control over journalists' careers? After all, reporters knew what had happened to Paul.

Ron Cannan, then a Kelowna city councillor and later a Conservative MP, wrote Paul a congratulatory letter. In it, he said he had urged reporters at the Capital News to publish a story about their former publisher winning a lawsuit against their former owners, Hollinger. A story did run, but the paper did not report on any other details. The article stated that the Capital News was at the present time owned by West Partners, a group of local businesspeople. It did not reveal that one of the partners was related to Vogt, the frontman for Horizon Operations.

It wasn't surprising that The Daily Courier did not want to touch a story that centred on a Hollinger loss. After all, its owner, Horizon Operations, was privately owned by Hollinger executives David Radler and Conrad Black. That had been revealed in Radler's testimony at the trial. The Kelowna TV station owned by CanWest, the company that at that time had just purchased all of Hollinger's big dailies in Canada, did not report the news, either – no report, despite having sent a reporter to almost every day of Paul's trial. The station, CHBC, even had a camera crew outside court at one point and had interviewed some of Paul's witnesses. We assume that nothing aired because Radler and Black were at that time on the CanWest board of directors.

To our utter relief and amazement, Hollinger's deadline to file an appeal came and went. We will never know why they suddenly let it go, but we suspect it had to do with the well written and tightly crafted decision by Judge Loo. We believe it left no room for appeal. Hollinger didn't have a leg to stand on, and Paul was thrilled that he and his "small-town lawyer" had outgunned the big guys.

The funds from Hollinger finally arrived in December 2002, three years after Paul's firing. The settlement, including legal costs and interest, totalled $211,000. This sounded pretty good, however there was a considerable difference between the formula for court-awarded costs and our actual legal expenses. Paul was remunerated for $28,000, but his legal and trial-related expenses ended up being about $112,000.

After paying the legal bill, income taxes, house sale and moving costs, and repaying employment insurance benefits, we were left with around $10,000.

"Alf Kempf was entitled to a share of my award based on our agreement. Given the time, energy and expertise he and his team put into my case, it was a reasonable amount," Paul agrees. "My issue was more with the court's extremely low formula for determining costs."

Some people wondered why Paul didn't claim punitive damages but he told them that although he was convinced his bosses wanted to punish him, his lawyer advised against it. Kempf was of the opinion that asking for them could have reduced our chance to win.

Had we lost the case, it would not have been pretty. In his Dale Carnegie course, Paul learned that one of the best ways to deal with the unknown is to prepare to accept the worst. Obviously, you expect the best but it's also critical to learn to accept the worst. For us, the worst would have been losing most, if not all, of the equity in our home. With the exception of some RRSPs, our other savings had been exhausted. Before the trial, we had borrowed $10,000 from my parents to keep us afloat. As very proud people, this had not been easy for us to do, especially because my dad, who was sympathetic to Paul's plight, was concerned that Hollinger would simply outspend us into submission.

Our Hollinger experience turned our world upside down, to put it mildly. Paul and I faced dramatic mid-life changes. At 49, when he should have been at the peak of his career, Paul found himself with lots of spare time. Running our small, hobby magazine company did not demand the 50 to 60 hours a week he had historically put in. This allowed me, however, to jump headlong into a new career. I had loved being a reporter and writer, but I was jaded and needed a change. Beyond that, we knew that it would be unwise for both of our careers and incomes to depend on the publishing business. At 44, I was accepted into the teacher pre-service program at Brock University.

Our friends and families were relieved and impressed that our battle had ended triumphantly. Paul truly appreciated the handful of congratulatory notes and phone calls from close personal friends. The one that probably meant the most to him was from Morgan Fisher, his former high-school marketing teacher and mentor. Fisher, who has since passed, wrote on August 23, 2002:

> *Congratulations on your successful battle with Hollinger. The K-W Record had a very prominent article in their Business Section. I have no doubt that your mother has already informed you of this detail. It takes a special person to have the courage to take on a huge conglomerate like Hollinger with its immense legal resources. You must have wondered over the past few years whether the time, expense and effort were worth it. I wish I could take credit for the high business ethics that you displayed in this case. However, I know the credit is due to your mother, a truly exceptional woman. Once again, you have given me much pleasure as I have watched your career develop. Once again, I am proud to be able to call you 'my student.'*

Life returned to normal for me as I moved ahead with my new career and put the Hollinger pain behind us. Paul, though, was not willing to sweep what he knew under the carpet and stay silent. So, he switched his focus from urging Canadian media to follow up on to alerting securities authorities about what his court case had revealed.

Paul decided that notifying officials at any one of several securities commissions would be the best opportunity to see justice truly served in this affair. After Hollinger had paid his damages, he sent a letter to the B.C. Securities Commission. In an email in January 2003, he explained that he believed Conrad Black and David Radler might be in a conflict of interest and possible breach of their fiduciary responsibility as the top two executives of Hollinger because of their personal ownership of Horizon. He described what had taken place in Kelowna and his lawsuit, and provided a link to the judge's ruling.

Within a day or two, the B.C. Securities Commission wrote back saying Hollinger wasn't in its jurisdiction and that Paul's complaint should be sent to the Ontario Securities Commission. He contacted the OSC within a day and received a reply within 48 hours. The OSC said it had reviewed the material and saw no securities or regulatory issues to address. "They basically blew me off," Paul recalls, incredulously.

That was the lowest point for him. "I won my court case, but ultimately Radler and Hollinger won, because no one was going to hold them accountable for their actions."

He felt deflated. So much of what had driven Paul to go through the whole fight with Hollinger was his belief that he had a responsibility to expose the wrongdoing of some very powerful people. Moreover, they were the very people who are supposed to be the primary defenders of truth in our free society: the media, and specifically newspapers. Paul and I leaned on each other and on our faith in the belief that his battle – our battle – would somehow benefit society in general. Our experience would show that an average person can prevail against powerful forces and see justice served.

Paul had sent material to all sorts of media outlets, including the CBC, in his valiant attempt to expose what had happened. He also contacted a journalism school and a media watchdog organization. No one seemed to be interested. From the Competition Bureau years ago to the OSC and now the media, institutions in which Paul had always believed, were letting him down.

There was one glimmer of hope from the media. Soon after Paul's victory, documentary filmmakers Debbie Melnyk and Rick Caine called him for an interview. They told him that they were creating a film called "Citizen Black," about Conrad Black. They asked if Paul would be their first interview, in September 2002. Although it was satisfying to explain what had happened to him, we knew the documentary would not air for at least another year.

Bryden Winsby, a former editor of the Capital News, asked Paul if winning the lawsuit had turned out to be a Pyrrhic victory. At that point, Paul thought it had. He never regretted taking on the fight, but we did both think that victory would be far more satisfying and further reaching. We had prevailed, but at great costs monetarily and emotionally.

Albert Schweitzer said that the tragedy of life is what dies inside a man while he lives. Not only was Paul's career abruptly cut short, but his optimistic belief in our democratic institutions withered away. He became somewhat bitter and cynical. I believe something died inside my husband that year. Even being named by the Ontario Community Newspaper Association as one of the industry's top 50 leaders in the past 50 years left him feeling hollow and empty instead of proud.

Time marches on, though, and Paul successfully revamped Trajan, our small, hobby publishing company. He and his partners were pleased with the financial results. He no longer needed to work fulltime at the business, so he negotiated to work fewer hours in exchange for having his pay frozen. He got involved in community service when he joined the Fonthill Rotary Club. The club asked Paul to serve on the executive and within two years, he was appointed president.

Volunteer work distracted him and it was fulfilling, but he simply could not shake off the pain of being ignored. No one seemed to be taking seriously what his trial had revealed. He felt like a stranger, an alien in his own land. He was about to give up trying to expose the wrongdoing when, one warm July evening in 2003, he got a call from a Chicago Tribune reporter.

XV

AMERICANS TO THE RESCUE

"It is in your moments of decision that your destiny is shaped."

- Tony Robbins

The phone rang while Paul and I were preparing supper and sipping on some wine. I had just graduated from Brock University's Faculty of Education that spring, and it was almost one year after Paul had won his lawsuit. I answered the call. The voice at the other end introduced himself as Jim Miller, a reporter from the Chicago Tribune. He asked if this was the residence of the same Paul Winkler who had successfully sued Hollinger for wrongful dismissal. I almost said, "Yeah, right; good one, Ken," thinking former newspaper colleague and now good friend Ken Bosveld was pulling my leg.

Bosveld has a real knack for imitating voices, but the caller's mid-west American twang sounded too authentic. Suspiciously, I passed the receiver to Paul and told him who the caller claimed to be. I silently cheered when I realized, from Paul's end of the conversation, that this was no joke.

After he hung up, Paul told me that Miller had called out to his boss, "I'm flying to Canada tomorrow." Thrilled at this turn of events, Paul took his files to the office and, true to his word, Miller showed up in St. Catharines the next day. At the time, The Tribune was competing against the Hollinger-owned Chicago Sun Times. The front-page story about Paul, published on Sunday, July 20, 2003, cast a light on the questionable dealings surrounding Radler and Black's personal ownership of Horizon.

Just one month prior to Paul's interview, Hollinger shareholders and board members representing investment businesses Tweedy, Browne & Co. and Cardinal Capital had been asking questions of Hollinger's top executives about the non-compete payments those men personally received when papers were sold. An investigation had been launched, opening a Pandora's box. This marked the beginning of the end for Black and Radler.

The headline on The Tribune story was "Hollinger newspaper sales raise questions: Black's holdings, actions give rise to conflict claims." Reporters James Miller and Jim Kirk led their article with: "Paul Winkler was feeling good about the success of his little newspaper in rural British Columbia." They wove Paul's legal battle and ultimate victory within the bigger story of Hollinger's American institutional shareholders wanting more details about the Horizon transactions.

The media avalanche about Black and Radler began with that article and quickly gained momentum. Suddenly, reporters couldn't seem to get enough of Paul. What a difference four years made. It became a feeding frenzy as Canadian media covered the corporate skullduggery from every possible angle. The Globe and Mail published a full-page piece outlining what happened to Paul in Kelowna and numerous other articles quoting him. Paul gave interviews to CBC Radio and TV. Significant stories ran in The Vancouver Sun and The National Post. Those were then sent out over the wires and run by other Canadian papers. Even The New York Times and The Wall Street Journal interviewed Paul as part of their coverage of the Hollinger executives' fall from grace.

The British were interested, too, because Hollinger International owned the Daily Telegraph, its sister paper The Sunday Telegraph, and The Spectator in the U.K. Black had renounced his Canadian citizenship in 2001 in order to become a British citizen and assume a peerage as Lord Black of Crossharbour. The Times of London interviewed Paul, as did BBC TV who flew a crew to Canada to cover the story. They even came to our house to get some footage.

Some of Paul's interviews focused on how the Ontario Securities Commission had blown off his complaint a year earlier. People now started to question how effective securities enforcement was in Canada. This was intensified because renowned investor Stephen Jarislowsky had also complained to the OSC about Hollinger's top executives.

In late 2003, when Paul heard that the Securities and Exchange Commission in the United States had launched its own investigation of Hollinger, he sent them an email offering his assistance. Paul remembers, "Unlike the OSC, the SEC got back to me right away requesting all the information I had. They followed that up with a lengthy phone interview involving a number of lawyers and an accountant in Chicago."

When OSC staff read about Paul's SEC interview in The Globe and Mail, they finally contacted him directly and asked if he would provide them with the same information he had given to the Americans. Paul complied, but no OSC representative ever interviewed him.

Before 2003 came to an end, Conrad Black, once a mighty force in the Canadian business establishment, resigned as CEO of Hollinger International. In January 2004, Hollinger International sued Black and Radler for $200 million over alleged financial irregularities. Black returned the favour, suing Hollinger International directors for $850 million for defamation. Hollinger International directors shot back, upping the ante by further alleging that Black, Radler and some associates were engaged in racketeering. If successful, Hollinger International could seek triple the damages under U.S. law.

A Special Committee of Hollinger International issued a 513-page document labelled "Corporate Kleptocracy" on August 31, 2004, claiming that Radler and Black had siphoned off more than $400 million from their publicly traded company. Weeks after the document's release, Black filed a $1.1 billion defamation lawsuit against the Special Committee.

That fall, Black resigned as chairman and CEO of Hollinger Inc., the Canadian-based parent company. He and Radler were completely turfed from the board weeks later, by order of a Superior Court Judge.

For the second year in a row, Black had the dubious honour of being named by The Canadian Press and Broadcast News as the Canadian business newsmaker of the year.

The "Corporate Kleptocracy" document, otherwise known as the "Hollinger Chronicles" or the "Breeden Report," fascinated Paul because it contained considerable detail surrounding the Horizon and Hollinger dealings in Kelowna. Included were interviews with David Black, Todd Vogt, Hollinger Executive V.P. Peter Atkinson, and contacts at the Competition Bureau. On page 327, under the title "The Kelowna Transactions," the report stated:

The Special Committee has determined that there were numerous fiduciary duty breaches surrounding certain Horizon-related transactions in Kelowna, a city located in British Columbia's Okanagan region. These transactions provide a vivid illustration of the manner in which Black's and Radler's conflicting loyalties to Hollinger and Horizon damaged Hollinger even when the Company was not selling newspaper assets directly to Horizon.

Paul was interested to read the interview with David Black of Black Press:

Black told the special committee that in 1998 he had made an offer to Radler to buy Hollinger's Kelowna Capital (News). At the same time, he was also trying to buy Thomson's Kelowna Daily. His plan was to acquire both Kelowna papers and consolidate them. Radler told David Black in 1998 that Hollinger would sell him the Kelowna Capital at a reasonable price. David Black then negotiated with Thomson to purchase the Kelowna Daily, ultimately entering into a written agreement to buy it for approximately $12.2 million.

Soon thereafter, Radler told David Black that Hollinger would not sell him the Kelowna Capital. This caused David Black to back out of his deal with Thomson to buy the Kelowna Daily. The Special Committee has found no evidence that Radler or anyone else ever informed Hollinger's independent directors of David Black's offer to purchase Hollinger's Kelowna Capital.

Paul said, "I was perplexed when I read David Black's interview. David told me after my dismissal in January 2000 that the Competition Bureau told him he couldn't own the two newspapers in Kelowna. It didn't make sense to me. Perhaps he learned that only after Radler had quashed the deal."

Regardless, the report made clear to Paul that Radler decided that rather than facilitate David Black's consolidation of newspapers in Kelowna, he wanted do it on his own, cutting out not only the Hollinger shareholders but also constructing the deal to ensure he personally reaped more of the gains than Conrad Black. We learned in this report that Radler actually owned almost 49 per cent of Horizon's shares, a far cry from the 24 per cent he testified to at Paul's trial. That would become an issue.

The report also outlined what happened to Paul, noting that six months after Horizon purchased The Daily Courier:

Winkler left his position as General Manager of Hollinger's Kelowna Capital. Around that time, Winkler informed the Competition Bureau that Horizon was a mere front for Radler and that the two Kelowna papers were not competing fairly.

Peter Atkinson, Executive V.P. of Hollinger International, said in the report that the Competition Bureau was upset when it learned that Black and Radler controlled both Kelowna papers. Eventually, the Bureau directed Radler to sell one of the two:

Atkinson's recollection is consistent with the March 19, 2002 affidavit of Competition Bureau law officer Paul Feuer. According to Feuer, the Bureau sought and reviewed documents relevant to Hollinger's and Horizon's ownership throughout 2000. The Bureau concluded that 'six senior executives of Hollinger collectively controlled a majority of the voting shares of Horizon and therefore the Kelowna Daily Courier.' Feuer and another officer met with Atkinson and told him that 'this common ownership raised a serious likelihood of substantially lessening or preventing competition in the market for print advertising in Kelowna.' On December 7, 2000, Atkinson advised the Bureau that Hollinger would 'act on a voluntary basis to address the[se] concerns' by 'divest[ing] either the [Kelowna] Capital News or the [Kelowna] Daily Courier to an arm's length purchaser within three months of January 1, 2001.

Even though David Black had made an offer to buy the Capital News in the fall of 2000, the Special Committee found that no one at Hollinger knew about it. The Breeden Report said:

On November 20, 2000, about two months after David Black's $7.4-8.1 million offer for the Kelowna Capital, West Partners offered to purchase all assets of Hollinger's Kelowna Capital and its affiliated publications, along with the Vernon Sun Review, for $5.4 million.

What Paul had suspected all along, but what had never been made public, was now revealed in the Special Committee report. We discovered that West Partners did rather well by their brief foray into the newspaper business.

West Partners has strong ties with Vogt. It is a partnership composed of Darryl Laurent (Vogt's stepfather), Bruce Hamilton (owner of the Kelowna Rockets hockey team), and Dave Dakers (General Manager of the Skyreach Place arena in Kelowna). According to West Partners' representations to its lender TD Bank and to the Competition Bureau, Darryl Laurent was West Partners' majority owner in January 2001 and, as recently as March 2002, owned 520 West Partners shares, while Hamilton and Dakers each owned 240 shares. Vogt stated in an affidavit to the Competition Bureau that he had known Hamilton and Dakers 'socially' for several years and [had] 'encouraged Mr. Dakers to invest with Mr.

*Hamilton in The [Kelowna] Capital News and the Vernon Sun Review.'
In fact, Vogt said that he had planned initially to leave Horizon and
become an investor in and executive of West Partners. In addition to bro-
kering the deal, he acknowledged that he performed due diligence on West
Partners' behalf and dealt with TD Bank on West Partners' behalf on its
loan application.*

*The Special Committee has not found direct evidence that either Vogt or Ra-
dler ever owned or controlled West Partners, or were paid by West Partners,
other than various suspicious circumstances, including: (i) Vogt's stepfather
owning a majority of West Partners; and (ii) Radler's willingness to sell to
West Partners a Hollinger newspaper that (a) Vogt had sought for Horizon,
and (b) Radler was unwilling to sell to David Black at a higher price.*

The committee's report stated that two years after West Partners
acquired the Capital News for approximated $5 million, it flipped that
property, as well as the Vernon Sun Review, to David Black for $13.7
million and $213,000, respectively.

Paul laments, "Add in about $2 million of operating profit per year
for the two years they owned it and you've got pre-tax gains of over $12
million. Not bad, given that your only qualification for this benefit was
either being related to Todd Vogt or being a friend of his."

The report shed light on the real relationship between Radler and
Vogt, one that was completely opposite what each had presented. Vogt
is quoted extensively throughout the Hollinger Chronicles. Paul suspects
that Vogt cooperated with the Special Committee to avoid any possible
action against him.

*Vogt maintains that he was upset initially when he learned that he would be
working for Horizon, and told Radler that he did not want to leave Hollinger.
He ultimately became President of Horizon, only because Radler, his boss
and mentor, insisted. Throughout his tenure as Horizon's president, Vogt was
supervised by and took instructions from Radler.*

136

*The Special Committee finds that Radler made this misrepresentation delib-
erately to mislead the Board into believing that he and Black would only be
passive, minority investors in Horizon. As Radler knew, Horizon would be
essentially his and Black's own newspaper company.*

Citing Paul's trial, wherein Radler stated that he owned only 24 per
cent of Horizon, the report says this was misleading because Vogt's holdings, known as Vee Holdings, were minimal:

*Radler knew that this testimony was false, because he knew that the Vee Hold-
ings nominee arrangement rendered his and Black's combined voting interest
at approximately 73%, not 48%, and that because of the Vee Holdings
voting trust, Vogt's voting interest was only about 6%, not anywhere near
'the thirties.' Radler also testified that he had no participation in Horizon's
management and that when Horizon was established in 1999, 'we [Black
and Radler] wanted him [Vogt] to be totally independent,' and that 'I [Ra-
dler] wanted him [Vogt] to have total control.' This was flat out false, and is
contradicted not only by the Declaration of Trust but also by Vogt himself, who
repeatedly stated during interviews with the Special Committee that he took
instructions from Radler while working at Horizon.*

Paul was pleased to read the passage:

*Radler gave false and misleading testimony about his Horizon ownership in-
terest during the January 2002 trial of Paul Winkler v. Lower Mainland
Publishing Ltd., a wrongful termination action brought by a former Hollinger
employee.*

To the best of our knowledge, the information in the Breeden Report is accurate. Conrad Black did take issue with various parts of the
report and sued for defamation. He reached an out of court settlement
with the authors in 2011. The complete report is still posted on the SEC
website.

Armed with the report, Paul wanted to get answers as to why the Competition Bureau had allowed his former paper to be sold to Vogt's stepfather, Daryl Laurent, along with Hamilton and Dakers.

First Paul phoned and then emailed the Bureau's Andre Brantz. Zeroing in on the report's statement that Vogt had brokered the deal selling majority ownership in the Capital News to his stepfather, Paul's email said how disappointed he was this sale had been allowed to take place. Paul urged the Bureau to take action since it seemed to Paul they may not have been aware of the link between Vogt and West Partners' controlling shareholder Darryl Laurent, Vogt's stepfather. When Paul did not receive a reply, he re-sent the email to Brantz. Still no response.

In the summer of 2004, Paul was contacted by Dianne Urquart, a well-known shareholder-rights activist. At her urging, he sent a letter to Ontario's Standing Committee on Financial and Economic Affairs, outlining his concerns over securities enforcement.

Six months later, Paul was asked to appear before a Senate Committee looking into media ownership. He pointed out how insular the Canadian media scene was and his assumption that most owners had known there was hanky-panky going on in Kelowna but no one protested because it was an Old Boys' club. He also explained it was impossible to know who actually owned Horizon. Paul further took the opportunity to point a finger at the Competition Bureau for inconsistent enforcement and unclear policies when it came to owning more than one newspaper in a community. Following his appearance, the committee made a recommendation for greater ownership transparency.

Eventually, the media attention subsided. Paul turned his focus to our publishing company and I worked hard to obtain a permanent teaching contract. However, my husband was still on the edge of his seat. On November 15, 2004, the U.S. Securities and Exchange Commission (SEC) laid criminal charges against Conrad Black and David Radler, accusing the two of using Hollinger as their personal piggy bank. Paul wondered if he would be called to testify. He was convinced the duo would serve time for their actions, something most others thought would never happen.

XVI

LETTING GO AND LESSONS LEARNED

"Happiness is not the absence of problems, it's the ability to deal with them." - Steve Maraboli, Life, the Truth and Being Free

Paul thought he might be called upon to testify at Conrad Black's trial in Chicago. Having spent almost four days on the witness stand at his own wrongful dismissal case, Paul felt confident in a courtroom setting. He told me he would not hesitate to go and give evidence, and was excited at the prospect. He had a judgment against Hollinger, and had provided testimony as part of the U.S. Securities and Exchange Commission's investigation.

Then, in a move that surprised us as well as many others, Radler pleaded guilty. In September 2005, almost one year after being charged, Black's partner struck a deal with prosecutors pleading guilty to one charge of fraud in exchange for his testimony against Black. Radler agreed to a 29-month prison sentence and a $250,000 fine. He eventually paid back almost $100 million to Hollinger. With Radler no longer facing charges, Paul knew he wouldn't be called to testify.

One newspaper described Radler as the faithful servant who turned the tables on his long-time business partner, in exchange for this sweetheart deal from the feds. While that may be true, Paul has a different theory he often shares with others. Paul thinks that because both Radler and Black were "caught with their fingers in the cookie jar," as co-defendants, everything alleged in Hollinger board's 513-page "Corporate

Kleptocracy" document could be used against them, along with anything the SEC uncovered on its own.

"I find it possible that Radler and Black decided the best way to minimize the fallout would be to have Radler plead guilty and turn government witness. Clearly the SEC wanted Conrad, the name-brand top dog, and I suspect they weren't as interested in his partner, Radler. It turns out that much of the alleged wrongdoing involved Radler more directly than Conrad Black and it was unlikely those deeds would be used against Black in court. Whether my theory is correct or not, I can't help thinking Radler's guilty plea reduced not only his own, but Conrad's, prison time, too," Paul says.

Radler testified against Conrad Black at Black's trial in Chicago in 2007. Black's well-known Canadian lawyer, Eddie Greenspan, positioned Radler as an unreliable witness. He accused Radler of perjury because he had lied under oath at Paul's wrongful dismissal trial. Radler also admitted under cross-examination that he lied on 10 separate occasions to 24 FBI agents, as well as to prosecutors and personnel from internal revenue and postal inspections.

Following his four-month trial, Conrad Black was found guilty on one charge of obstruction and three charges of mail fraud. He was sentenced to six and a half years in prison. On appeal, in 2011, two of the mail fraud convictions were overturned and his sentence was reduced to just less than four years. He therefore spent one more year in jail and was released on May 4, 2012.

Radler reported to a prison in Pennsylvania on February 25, 2008, and served seven months before being turned over to Canadian authorities to complete his sentence. He served three months in a Canadian facility and was released on December 15, 2008, based on the grounds that he was unlikely to commit a violent act. He served fewer than 10 months of the 29 to which he had been sentenced.

Paul, on the other hand, had paid a steep price for not cooperating with Hollinger and his bosses' plans for the Kelowna marketplace. Even though he wasn't behind bars, he often compares his post-Kelowna experience to serving jail time. He lamented for many years losing his career in a business for which he had so much passion, and leaving a community to which our family had become emotionally attached. Despite those hardships, he has never regretted his decision to stay true to his values and has gained much satisfaction from that resolve. Driven by a deep sense of personal, business and journalistic duty to promote transparency and truth telling, Paul felt he was fighting not just for himself and his family but also for his staff, and most importantly, for the newspaper industry.

To help with the healing process and to let go of negativity and anger, many who feel they have been wronged, are counseled to forgive. We really haven't had the chance to forgive because we haven't received any apologies but Paul did something many might think odd. "I used to pray for David Radler while on my runs in Kelowna," Paul remembers. "It really helped reduce my feelings of outrage and exasperation."

Paul struggled to find meaning in his new role as publisher of Trajan, our small publishing company in St. Catharines. Going to work every day without fervour and passion took its toll on him emotionally. He had many private dialogues with God, wondering if something positive would come from his stand. Would he find a sense of purpose, passion and direction again?

He took some solace in getting parts of his story written in various newspaper articles and reported on several radio and TV programs mainly in 2003 and 2004. "Reporters were eager to dig further into Black and Radler's dealings once it became a big story. I was willing to help them but still felt the pain of having been ignored earlier," Paul says. Also, British author Tom Bower interviewed Paul for his book Conrad and Lady Black: Dancing on the Edge published in 2006, and about six years later, Bruce Livesey called to interview Paul for his book, Thieves of Bay Street. Livesey devoted much of Chapter 15 to Paul's story.

Paul operated our small publishing company for 12 years, selling our shares in 2013. After a rocky start, Trajan turned out to be more economically successful than he expected and for that we were both very grateful.

For my part, I considered the Hollinger affair one huge bump in the rocky road of life. I looked positively toward the future and then, in 2002, decided to apply to Brock University to become a teacher. Paul often tells people that I was the real hero going back to school full time and starting over in a new career. I am flattered when he says that but, while it took courage to take the academic plunge, I don't feel like a hero.

Most importantly, the adventure solidified our relationship and demonstrated our marriage vows in action to our children and others. We believed in each other. We supported each other. Above all, we trusted each other. Speaking in broad societal terms, the experience confirmed for us, without a doubt, the absolute need for all of us to be trustworthy people if we hope to continue to enjoy the quality of life we've come to know in the western world.

Trustworthy describes someone you can rely on to be honest or truthful. Trustworthy people have integrity. They integrate truth into their lives. They do the right thing even when no one is watching. Integrity is not hit or miss and cannot be abandoned when convenient.

In Paul's case, he told his staff in Kelowna that his priority was to ensure that everyone on the team was trustworthy. He made a big deal about it. "So much can be accomplished by a group of individuals when you create the right environment, and that starts with trust. When team members know what's to be accomplished collectively, and their role in the big picture, good things happen. Moving in the right direction breaks down if one's co-workers aren't doing their part. That's why management must have the ability to deal with those people quickly and decisively. When everyone is aligned and rowing in the same direction, it's almost magical. We had that at the Capital News for a couple of years and saw incredible growth and had so much fun."

Paul recoiled when he was asked to do things that he saw as breaking a contract of trust with his staff. He knew if he complied with his bosses, he would be duplicitous. As a businessman, Paul was regarded as tough-minded with a strong bottom-line focus, but he also embraced the core values of caring, honesty, respect, and responsibility. He read and put into practice the philosophies outlined in Stephen Covey's book, Principle-Centered Leadership. Many of those principles mirror the Christian upbringing that both Paul and I experienced and try to model for our children.

We have observed some interesting reactions to our story. Paul notes, "Many people under the age of 40 are not familiar with Conrad Black, and those who are don't seem to know how to respond, especially when I mention that I was, in effect, a whistleblower. Very few commended me for having done something worthwhile and those who did were often older people. Someone told me whistleblowers are not looked upon favourably because they are viewed as tattletales or self-righteous."

We don't think that what Paul did should be considered heroic or out of the ordinary. We would like to think that most of us would do the same. It is disheartening, then, to find that so many people view what he did as being foolish and reckless; especially when they find out he was about to be promoted. One senior editor at a national newspaper said in a letter to me he admired Paul's courage and admitted he would not likely have risked his job doing what Paul did.

Most people consider themselves to be truthful and honest. The real test comes when we are called to sacrifice something to uphold those values. It seems to us that fewer people are willing to make sacrifices and, as a result, moral standards are slipping. There's more emphasis on "doing things right" instead of "doing the right thing." Some clearly think a crime is only a crime if there's a reasonable chance you'll get caught.

We hope our story inspires readers to take pause and think of their own principles. Writing this memoir and making ourselves available to speak to interested groups will be the something positive that comes out of the horrible chapter in our lives.

Philosopher Emile Durkheim may have been stating it strongly when he said, "when *mores* are sufficient laws are not necessary, when *mores* are insufficient, laws are unenforceable." But we think he says so to warn us that if the majority no longer plays by the rules, chaos will result and then laws are really difficult to enforce.

We know what kind of society we want. Do you?

WHERE ARE THEY NOW?

Radler continues to own and operate newspapers through several privately controlled companies. His Alberta Newspaper Group Ltd. owns the Lethbridge Herald, the Medicine Hat News, the Sherbrooke Record, and dozens of smaller publications. He also has Continental Newspapers, which owns three dailies: the Thunder Bay Chronicle, The Daily Courier in Kelowna, and the Penticton Herald. He is in partnership with Glacier Media. Interestingly, two of the principals in Glacier are the heads of Madison Venture Corporation, the company that controlled LMPL when Paul was hired in 1996 to head up its Okanagan papers. Glacier owns the Victoria Times Colonist and, to the shock of many insiders, appointed Radler as its acting publisher in March 2013.

In September 2011, the Chicago Sun Times reported that Black sued Radler for breach of fiduciary responsibility, in a suit that alleges Radler hurt the value of Black's stake in Horizon Publications Inc. There has been no news on that front at the time of writing our book.

After being released from federal custody in 2012, Conrad Black returned to live in Toronto under a temporary residency permit. He lost a bid in February 2013 to void his conviction on fraud and obstruction charges on grounds that he was blocked from hiring the defense lawyers he wanted.

In 2013, the former media baron began co-hosting a weekly television show for the over-50 set called The Zoomer – Television for Boomers with Zip. The talk show airs on Vision TV and Black has interviewed guests who include embattled Toronto mayor Rob Ford.

Also in 2013, the Ontario Securities Commission said it would revive its case against Black that had been on hold since 2005 pending resolution of his criminal case and subsequent appeals. Black's lawyer was trying to have the case thrown out early in 2014.

On January 31, 2014, Governor General David Johnston, on the recommendation of the Advisory Council of the Order of Canada, terminated Conrad Black's appointment as an Officer of the Order of Canada. The former media mogul was also removed from The Queen's Privy Council of Canada.

We have not heard much about David Dodd, Paul's boss when Hollinger took over LMPL in 1998. He was working in the Chicago area for Hollinger in 2002 and likely finished his newspaper career in that city, when Radler and Black were removed from the company, in 2004.

Todd Vogt kept a low profile after leaving Horizon shortly after Paul's trial in 2002. He likely wasn't hurting for cash, given the millions his father-in-law made as controlling shareholder of the Capital News, in a deal Vogt engineered. His profile shot back up in dramatic fashion when he teamed up with David Black of Black Press, based in Victoria. They're partners in the San Francisco Newspaper Company and own papers in that city, including the San Francisco Examiner, a free daily. "Why David Black would partner with Vogt is beyond explanation in my mind," Paul remarks.

In early 2013, a competing publication, San Francisco Magazine, published a feature profile piece on Vogt, describing him as brash and someone who had gone out of his way to make himself notorious. The article said Vogt "launched a one-man Twitter campaign against House Minority Leader Nancy Pelosi (who represents the area) and takes regular swipes at the other local newspapers."

ABOUT THE AUTHOR

Mary Lynn McCauley Winkler has a Bachelor of Journalism and Bachelor of Education. She is a former broadcast and print journalist and now an elementary school French teacher with the District School Board of Niagara. This is her first book. She lives with her family in Fonthill, Ontario.

Made in the USA
Charleston, SC
26 August 2014